Hidden Worlds of Wildlife

25th Anniversary Edition. This book belongs to

amie Allrecht

Name   Date

ZOO

ZOO
The Modern Ark

Photographs by
Franz Maier

Text by
Jake Page

Preface by
Gerald Durrell

KEY PORTER·BOOKS

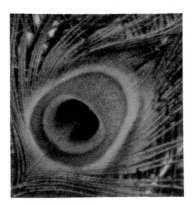

Canadian Cataloguing in Publication Data

Maier, Franz
  Zoo : the modern ark

ISBN 1-55013-208-3

1. Zoos. 2. Zoos · History.   I. Page, Jake.

II. Title.

QL76.M34 1990   590'.74'4   C89-095188-8

Key Porter Books Limited
70 The Esplanade
Toronto, Ontario
M5E 1R2

Design: Marie Bartholomew
Typesetting: Q Composition Inc.

Printed and bound in Hong Kong

90 91 92 93 94 6 5 4 3 2 1

Page 2
Gerald Durrell, founder of the Jersey Zoo, purchased the Zoo's first gorilla (*Gorilla gorilla*), a female, for £1,200. Its mate, Jambo, came later from the Basel Zoo where it was the first gorilla to be conceived and reared in captivity. The Jersey gorilla group is now well established and popular with visitors.

Contents

"The hippopotami in their tank at Central Park" by F.S. Church, *Harper's Weekly*, September 1888.

Preface

In recent years zoological gardens have been getting a lot of bad publicity due to criticism from well meaning but basically uninformed people. It is, of course, to be deplored that there are still a number of bad zoos in the world and they should be criticized in order that they will improve their standards. However, it is unfortunate that the great number of good zoos tend to be included with the bad ones and so the attitude of many people has come to be: if it is a zoo it must automatically be bad. The truth is a well conducted zoological garden can play an important role in our lives.

There is no substitute for the living animal. No pictures, films or photographs of an elephant, for example, can prepare you, or take the place of, your first meeting with such a spectacular creature. By studying the animals kept in zoos we learn more about the world we live in and, in consequence, more about ourselves. The enormous importance of the zoo's place in the conservation field has only just recently been recognized, even by the zoos themselves. As reservoirs and sanctuaries for endangered species it is impossible to over-emphasize their potential contribution. With the world being raped at such ferocious speed by mankind, with species vanishing almost hour by hour, zoos may well become the only place where large creatures, such as the elephant, the giraffe or the rhinoceros will exist in fifty years' time, to say nothing of a host of small creatures who are being harried to extinction by our activities.

The role of a zoological garden has changed radically in the last fifty years. No longer is it the Victorian menagerie where animals were incarcerated so that people could gawp and be amused by their antics or appearance. Zoos now (at least the best and most responsible ones) are saving creatures from extinction, breeding them, giving them — if you like — breathing space to renew their numbers and then putting them back into the wild.

Already this captive breeding has borne spectacular results. The Père David's deer, extinct in China, has been returned there from captive bred stock. The Przewalski horse has been reintroduced in the same way, as has the Arabian oryx, the Addax and many other creatures. We in Jersey have been instrumental in saving the pink pigeon of Mauritius and in the rehabilitation of Round Island in the Indian Ocean, which has more endangered species for its size than anywhere else in the world.

Zoological gardens, from ancient China and from the time of the Aztecs, have been with and are with us still. Zoos are not out of date. Indeed, they are becoming of greater importance with each passing year as this excellent book will show. The people who now criticize zoos should be calling not for their elimination, but for bigger and better ones.

Gerald Durrell
Honorary Director, Jersey Wildlife Preservation Trust

Prologue: Akbar's Problem

Among the traditional trappings of royalty and wealth, Akbar the Great possessed 1,000 cheetahs, those high-shouldered, spring-loaded predators that are the fastest known animal on land. Millennia earlier, cheetahs had adorned the gardens of the pharaohs and, prior to the sixteenth century, had roamed the royal grounds of innumerable leaders. Akbar presided over a region that now comprises most of India and Afghanistan and, although he was illiterate himself, he supported centers of learning in Delhi and Agra. A man with a passion for spiritual certainty, he promoted the Dini-i-Ilaha in 1560, a new divine faith to which his people paid allegience until Akbar's death in 1605, at which time they reverted to Islam. In fact, one of Akbar's few failures during his lifetime was the fact that his cheetahs would not breed.

Desperate, Akbar ordered his palace gardens open to the animals, possibly displaying an early insight that a free-ranging animal tends to experience less stress than a confined one and therefore is more likely to act naturally and breed. But, even with the run of the palace, the cheetahs proved uncooperative. They produced but one litter, the last cheetahs born in captivity until more than three centuries later (in 1956, a captive pair produced a litter in the Philadephia Zoo).

As a rule, zoos do not have patron saints; however, if they did, Akbar might well be chosen for that role: certainly the ancient potentate has the sympathy of any modern zoo director. Such people are, in a sense, spiritual descendants of Akbar and all the other great rulers in history who kept exotic animals among their retinues — back in time to the pharaohs and the Chinese mandarins 3,000 years ago, through to the Asian moguls and European royalty who had reserves set aside exclusively for their majesties' hunting.

Many zoos in Europe and elsewhere evolved from such reserves. Regency Park was a royal hunting preserve on the outskirts of London before it became the site of the world's first "modern" zoo. Most zoos today are enclaves within urban environments, some owing their location to the convenience of kings (who often resided in cities) or to the fact that cities are where the people are and, today, zoos need a different kind of patronage: a lot of visitors. It has been estimated that in the United States — famous for vast crowds attending football and other sports matches and visiting Disney World and its clones — zoo attendance figures are higher than those of any other component in the nation's recreational/cultural repertoire. And largely unbeknown to the millions who wander through the world's zoos, the last two decades have seen a profound and remarkable revolution in the nature of the zoo.

The most successful breeding group of cheetah (*Acinonyx jubatus*) in the world, with more than 120 recorded births, is at Whipsnade, in Bedfordshire, England. Jersey's cheetahs, one of which is shown here, are on loan from Whipsnade.

The modern zoo is beset by Akbar's age-old problem, but today there is a desperate urgency to finding its solution. Akbar, after all, could easily enough replenish his cheetah collection from the wild. Today, for many species, this is no longer an option. With the inexorable encroachment of mankind into their habitats, many wild animals survive as endangered species in reserves set aside for them — and in zoos. Indeed, the circle is nearly closed. For, from these exotic enclaves in some of the world's great cities, knowledge and techniques are being discovered that enable such reserves to be better managed and species better preserved. For millennia an "extractive industry," zoos are now learning how to repay the gift.

1 · The Revolutionary Zoo

In studying history, it is often difficult to find the straw that broke the camel's back, the event that triggered a revolution and led to a whole new way of thinking. But, in the long annals of zoological parks, one event can be reasonably pinpointed as having brought a number of growing trends into sharp focus to produce the single greatest change in zoos since man's prehistoric ancestors got the idea of digging a pit and — probably for religious purposes — keeping in it their ferocious totem/enemy, a cave bear. This revolutionizing event was the publication in a science journal of some seemingly dry statistics gathered by three young researchers at the National Zoological Park in Washington, D.C.

The article, published in *Science* magazine in 1979, was a straightforward correlation of juvenile mortality to inbreeding in sixteen species of ungulates, or grazing animals, that had been bred at the zoo: various species of deer, antelope, zebra, elephant, and pygmy hippo. For fifteen of the sixteen species, the facts were starkly clear: the death of young animals was markedly higher among inbred offspring than among noninbred offspring. The inbred young often died of starvation or medical problems, such as infections, not found among the noninbred.

The senior author of the article, Katherine Ralls, continued the study, extending her analysis to forty-four mammals in all, including a number of nonungulates, and announced the same sorry results

William T. Hornaday, the Smithsonian Institution's taxidermist, started the animal collection that became the National Zoological Park in Washington. He is shown here standing on the Mall with a buffalo calf, about 1887.

for 93 percent of the species. The implications were enormous, and the world of zoos reacted with remarkable speed.

In the decades before the Ralls study, most zoos had intensified their efforts to breed animals in captivity for the very reason that many zoo favorites were on endangered lists and replacement of zoo populations had to be accomplished without tapping wild resources. But small populations of a species — and any zoo population is small — are likely to become inbred, if they can be coaxed into breeding at all. One or two adults — called founders — can, over a generation or two, flood such a population with their genes. Breeders of plants, livestock and pets have long used inbreeding to create strains of creatures for special purposes; however, if inbreeding is continued for too long a time, it can lead to a number of congenital problems (one thinks of chronic hip dysplasia among some breeds of dog). But, equally insidious are the increases in juvenile mortality and the reduced fecundity that prolonged inbreeding produces. In part because zoo records of births and deaths tended to be few and scattered, it was not obvious until the Ralls studies that inbreeding was much of a problem in zoos.

That situation changed almost overnight. It became crystal clear that zoo populations had to be managed a new way: they had to be planned according to the sophisticated tenets of population genetics. More than that, zoos would have to cooperate with one another in unprecedented ways. If the silent stalker, inbreeding, was to be kept at bay, a zoo could no longer be content with managing its own little band of, say, Siberian tigers. Rather, all captive Siberian tigers in all the zoos of a continent — or even worldwide — had to be treated as a single population.

The traffic in many exotic species not only had to stop being a one-way street from the wild to individual zoos here and there but had to become multidirectional — between zoos. Once it was determined that a certain male tiger had sired the right number of cubs in one place, he would have to be moved to another zoo or prevented from breeding.

The Ralls study also had implications for those people engaged in managing wild populations of endangered species. More often than not, such populations are small and isolated: the same kind of inbreeding problems can conceivably stalk these animals as well. Intervention, in the form of genetic management, might well be needed in the wild. Indeed, it became reasonable to imagine that captive-bred animals from zoos might be introduced into wild habitats, perhaps to intermingle with their wild counterparts, thus strengthening their overall genetic viability.

Zoos, thus, had a new role, a qualitatively new task added on to the three goals that zoos have pursued since time immemorial: preparing a facility that works for the animal, the keeper, and the viewer. All animals need sustenance, of course, but a zoo animal also needs an enclosure of some sort, one that enables the keeper to tend to the animal. And the entire business is pointless if the viewer — be it a king and his noble cronies, or the public — cannot see the animal. All zoos, from the Stone Age bear pit to the modern zoo, have faced this triad of concerns. For the modern zoo, the goal of making the facility work for the animal has expanded into the realm of basic zoological research, while that of accommodating the viewer has broadened into elaborate educational programs. The story of zoos, until very recently, is one of evolution, not revolution.

It was not long after mankind learned to write on stone tablets that the first animal park was established, by a third-dynasty ruler of the Sumerian city of Ur around 2300 BC. A millennium later, civilization had sprouted widely throughout the Near East and Asia, and Assyrian rulers and pharaohs, despite their tendencies to wage war on each other, often exchanged exotic animals for each other's zoos. Assur's first great king, Tiglath-pileser I, sought animals from nearby lands and was given them as gifts or tribute. Ramses IX sent monkeys, crocodiles and what was listed as a "donkey of the water" — a hippopotamus. A pond was built at Assur for this "donkey"; large predators were kept in pits. A continent away, in China, the emperor Wu Wang of the Chou dynasty laid out a zoological garden called the Park of Intelligence. What seems to be the first recorded animal-collecting expedition was ordered by Egypt's Queen Hatshepsut around 1490 BC: a ship was sent south to the coast of what is now Somali, returning with exotic birds and monkeys for the royal animal park. Centuries later, royal animal parks flourished under the Ptolemies — but always as private reserves for the rulers and their noble guests. Cheetahs and lions were tamed and roamed the gardens. In the third century BC, Aristotle instituted what might be thought of as an experimental zoo, at any rate a private menagerie for his own observation. Perhaps influenced by this, the philosopher's pupil, Alexander the Great, having established the port of Alexandria in Egypt, installed what was probably the first public zoo.

African monkeys, lions, elephants, giraffes, and buffalo from Asia Minor were among the species featured in a zoo at Constantinople in AD 424. Closed pens housed the monkeys and lions, while the others had the run of large enclosures. In Antioch, a major commercial center and port, thousands of people each year visited a zoo located at the end of the main avenue of the city, until it was destroyed in 538 by the Persians.

In these ancient times, zoos were not the kind of systematic collections of animals that we have come to expect, but were usually more casual affairs — menageries. And, with few exceptions, notably the Chinese and Alexandrian animal parks, they were not created for the purpose of enlightenment so much as to display wealth and power or to provide exotic hunting for their founders. As it related to zoos, enlightenment, meaning learning and understanding, was a long way off. Entertainment was the function of most collections, and pitting exotic animals against each other in "baiting" arenas was often part of the zoo, nowhere more so than in the bloody amphitheaters of imperial Rome.

After the fall of Rome, and in the ensuing "dark ages" of Europe, it was chiefly monasteries that maintained the tradition of menageries and game parks. Charlemagne, however, kept, near his Aachen palace, a small zoo that included a tame lion, given to him by the pope, and an elephant, named Abul Abbas.

Four hundred years later, in the thirteenth century, Frederick II, the king of Sicily, established large menageries at Palermo and other cities and sent forth three traveling menageries elsewhere in Europe, possibly influencing other European rulers to establish zoological gardens or, as in Constantinople, to expand existing ones. The European discovery of the New World provided a great impetus to European zoodom. Ferdinand and Isabella of Spain, who had dispatched the Genoan sailor Columbus to find a westerly route to India, were soon pleased to stock their palace gardens with Cuban monkeys and parrots. King Manuel the Great of Portugal reveled in his Brazilian monkeys and macaws. But, it was in the New World itself where the most elaborate, and in some ways most civilized, zoo in the world existed.

On reaching the Aztec capital, Tenochtitlán, located in the middle of a great lake in central Mexico, the conquistador Cortes and his men were stunned to find a city that rivaled in architectural beauty and sophistication the finest cities of Europe. Virtually everywhere in the city were aviaries filled with brightly colored birds, the air alive with their song. And, set in a silvan park behind Emperor Montezuma's palace was a zoo unlike anything any European had ever imagined. Pens with bronze bars housed big cats — pumas and jaguars. The Spaniards saw sloths, monkeys, armadillos. Colorful fish inhabited six large basins, and huge snakes lived in sunken terraria; waterfowl plied ten separate ponds, tended by hundreds of "keepers." People were employed solely to collect cast-off feathers for making ceremonial robes. It took hundreds of turkeys each day to feed the captive eagles and hawks. (In a sorry precedent for the less-attractive menagerie/freak shows that would be popular later, the Aztecs also kept deformed people in the zoo, feeding them in the same manner as the wild animals.)

Two years later, in 1521, when Cortes, angry at the defiant Aztecs, returned and laid siege to the city, the starving inhabitants evidently survived for a time on the animals of the zoo and, when the conquerors finally took the city, they razed it, including the buildings of the animal park, and, in a last act of horrific contempt, torched the aviaries. Some of the trees survived and were still there evidently when, after more than 400 years, the Mexico City Zoo was established in this century.

As European explorers pried secrets from the heretofore hidden geography of the New World and such realms as Indonesia, their sponsors back home took to building animal parks with a vengeance. King Manuel of Portugal not only built his own zoo but profiteered from his control of the exotic-animal market, entertaining merchants with elephant parades in order to soften the blow of his ever-rising prices. The wealthy Fugger family, with its nearly global mercantile interests, established a zoo in Augsburg in 1570, populated with specimens from Africa and Central and South America. The Grand Duke of Tuscany was fascinated by exotics and would buy virtually any creature that arrived in his ports from abroad and put it in his animal park in Florence.

Perhaps the most enlightened zoos of the time, however, were not to be found in Europe but thousands of miles away, in India, where Akbar, whose cheetahs would not breed, was the Great Mogul. Toward the end of the sixteenth century, Akbar set up zoos in several Indian cities, with strong cages for the likes of lions, tigers and rhinos. When he died in 1605, his zoos contained 5,000 tame elephants and 1,000 dromedaries and camels. Himself of Mongol heritage, and said to be one of the most ethically enlightened rulers in history, Akbar shared the nomad tradition of love for animals: he forbade any form of animal baiting and, as had the Aztecs, employed people specially trained in what we now call veterinary medicine for his zoos. All of Akbar's zoos were open to the public.

Meanwhile, in Europe, the Habsburgs had established a zoo in Vienna, closed to the general public, except for the Viennese Baiting Theater where animals were, from time to time, set upon each other. (Mankind has a long history of this sort of thing. There is some speculation that chickens were first domesticated some 5,000 years ago for the purpose of cockfighting. Only later was it noticed that hens were reliable layers of nutritious eggs, and the ancient Egyptians established what could be thought of as chicken "factories.") In any event, Maria Theresa, who would become Empress of Austria, was much enamored of the zoo at Vienna; when she reached imperial status, she and her husband reinvigorated the zoo as the Imperial Menagerie at Schönbrun for the convenience and delight of Viennese courtiers and, later, burghers. There were twelve enclosures built around a central court; predators were kept in barred cages, game animals in cages open at the top. Later a garden pavilion was added. By modern standards it would have seemed claustrophobic, but it is said that a griffon vulture lived there for 117 years.

The winds of change were by then blowing briskly across Europe — political winds calling for democracy. In Paris, after the French Revolution, the Committee for Public Safety decreed that the former Jardin du Roi would be open to the public. By now it was called the Jardin des Plantes and was chiefly a botanical garden. (Botanical gardens evolved separately from zoos. They were places where plants could be studied by scientists to increase agricultural output.) After the Revolution, the great naturalist Baron Cuvier was installed to reorganize the Jardin into a zoo as well. An expert administrator as well as the leading anatomist of his time, Cuvier built up the Jardin des Plantes to the point where, after the fall of Napolean and his counterrevolutionary era, it was rivaled only by the zoo in Vienna.

It was, oddly enough, the democratization of Europe, along with

The Jardin des Plantes in Paris was originally a botanical garden. Exotic animals
were gradually introduced in the later decades of the nineteenth century. This
rendering of hippopotami in the Paris Zoo by F.S. Church appeared in *Harper's
Weekly* in April, 1870.

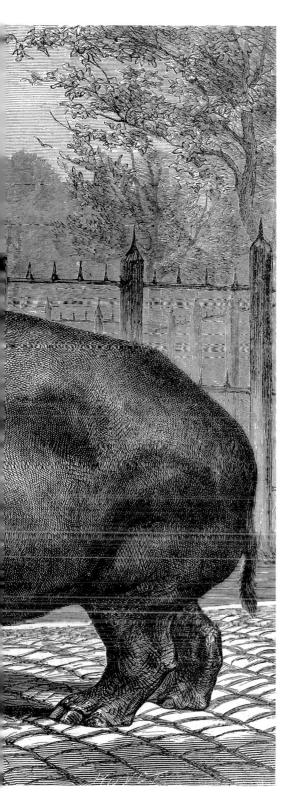

the rise of industrialization — the accumulation of great stores of capital in urban concentrations — that gave rise to what is called the "modern" zoo. There soon came into being the idea of a zoo as a repository of exotic specimens of life that were to be studied as a way of understanding the flora and fauna of lands now under the imperial hegemony of Europe. Public monies — rather than the whimsy of royal stipends — were now made available for zoos and liaisons with university faculties were instituted. The beginnings of this quantum leap in zoo development were present in Cuvier's reorganization in Paris, but the modern zoo is said to have come about in 1826 when the Zoological Society of London founded the zoological gardens at Regent's Park. The purpose was expressly the study of living animals to better understand the natural history of their wild counterparts in the far-flung realms of the British Empire. Veterinary care and post mortems were the norm, and once a zoo animal did die, it could be given to the British Museum (Natural History) for further study. Zoos had suddenly become part of the quest for knowledge.

A view of the London Zoo, Regent's Park, in 1835 by an unknown artist.

The idea spread quickly through Europe. A German explorer of Africa, Martin Lichtenstein, persuaded King Friedrich Wilhelm IV of Prussia to give his menagerie to the German people; thus was the Berlin Zoo founded in 1844, with one of the most celebrated naturalists of the era appointed as its director, Alexander von Humboldt. In 1874, far across the Atlantic, the Philadelphia Zoological Society opened the doors of the Philadelphia Zoo, America's first.

Characteristically, these first modern zoos were established in what we are pleased to call the Temperate Zone, where summers may be hot and winters intemperately cold; therefore, the tropical species that were often the most popular attractions for the public had to be housed in buildings that could be heated. Thus came into being massive, steam-heated artificial life-support systems. Indoor aviaries and huge mammal houses (only rarely with adjacent outdoor yards) became the style of the time in zoos. Because of the fear of disease, which could quickly wipe out expensive animal collections, these buildings had cement floors and tiled walls, that could be easily hosed down, a far cry from anything found in nature. Today, we tend to cringe at such enclosures: at the time they were the best good minds could contrive to protect the life of the animal, to facilitate the work of the keeper, and to cater to the interests of the viewer.

And, of course, the interests of the viewer, in the new age of public zoos, became an increasingly important consideration. To operate a zoo, a zoological society had to raise funds, since the cost of such an undertaking would be beyond the means of a few science-minded patrons. So, whether funds were to come from public or private sources, the zoo — however lofty its goals for research and, later, conservation — had first to be a popular attraction. Much attention had to be paid to what, today, zoo people call (with a certain irony) "charismatic megafauna": big (ferocious) cats, big (performing) elephants, big (monstrous) rhinos, big (improbable) giraffes, big (dangerous) bears, and so forth.

In the nineteenth century the London Zoo, in common with most other zoos, combined some elements of the circus menagerie with its more serious, scientific pursuits. Rides on the famous bull African elephant, Jumbo, were one such feature when this photograph was taken, about 1872. Jumbo was subsequently sold to P.T. Barnum's circus.

Carl Hagenbeck, shown here in a photograph taken about 1910, introduced a new concept of zoo design when he founded his private zoo in Stellingen, Germany. Bars, pits and cages were, to the greatest possible extent, replaced by moats, ditches and other, less distracting barriers.

William Mann cut a dashing figure between the wars. As superintendent of the National Zoological Park in Washington D.C., he made a number of animal collecting expeditions to exotic places. Here he is shown accompanied by his wife, Lucy, on the St. Paul's River in Liberia in 1940.

It was during the nineteenth century, when the modern zoo was coming into its own that Frederick II's Sicilian legacy also reached full bloom. In North America and Europe the traveling menagerie was a very popular feature. Such traveling shows, combining exotic animals and exotic human performances, brought excitement to remote regions of the American frontier long before cities sprang up and, with them, boosters that decided any city worth its salt needed, among other things, its own permanent zoo. The lines between traveling menagerie, circus and zoo often became blurred in those days. It was an escapee from such a menagerie — evidently a chimpanzee — that made history in the Pacific Northwest by being mistaken for Bigfoot, a legendary half-man/half-ape that is said to roam those forested vastnesses to this day, leaving gigantic, enigmatic footprints in its wake. Now, that would be a zoo specimen!

Indeed, zoos became quite competitive in their quests for attractive superlatives. The wealthiest zoos took to mounting their own animal-collecting expeditions, often accompanied by great fanfare, and occasionally accompanied by intrigue worthy of Hollywood. The Western quest for that enigmatic jewel of the Middle Kingdom, China's giant panda, is a case in point.

The first Westerner to lay eyes on a giant panda was the French missionary and naturalist Père Armand David. In 1869, David's party of hunters in the high bamboo forests of Szechuan shot a young specimen of what was locally called the white bear. David named it *Ursus melanoleuca*, meaning "black and white bear," and with an adult specimen that was shot shortly afterwards, sent it off to the Paris Museum of Natural History where Professor Henri Milne-Edwards announced that, while the animal had a bear-like outward appearance, its internal anatomy showed that it was more closely related

In 1929, two of former us president Theodore Roosevelt's sons, Theodore Junior and Kermit, embarked on an expedition to central Asia. Two of their "captures," a pair of giant pandas, subsequently made their appearance in this diorama, which is still on display in the Field Museum of Natural History in Chicago.

Theodore Roosevelt set out in 1909 on the Smithsonian-Roosevelt Africa Expedition to collect and send back animals for display in the National Zoological Park in Washington, D.C.

to the raccoon. Thus was set off a debate that has been resolved only in the last decade (the panda is more closely related to the bear). But, the giant panda's arrival in Paris also set off an explosion of interest among scientists and the public. Before long the giant panda was considered the rarest and most desirable sporting trophy in the world. Many set out to shoot one, and many failed. In the late 1920s, two sons of former U.S. president Theodore Roosevelt, Teddy Jr. and Kermit, set forth, vowing that they would not return from the difficult mountain terrain of Szechuan until they had bagged one of these rare creatures. As it turned out, they captured two, which wound up stuffed at the Field Museum in Chicago, an addition to scientific knowledge and a source of much publicity for the Roosevelt brothers. Eventually several more pandas were shot to satisfy the appetites of science and sport.

In 1934, however, the notion of bringing a live panda out of China gleamed in the eyes of two animal collectors. Tangier Smith of Shanghai, an old China hand; and William Harkness, Jr., of New York, who had already supplied the Bronx Zoo with some very charismatic Komodo dragons. Two weeks before he left for China, Harkness married a New York dress designer, whom he promptly left behind. Almost two years later, his expedition nothing more than a string of mishaps and frustrations, Harkness died in Shanghai of a mysterious illness and his wife, Ruth, improbably, decided to pursue his ambition.

Reaching Shanghai in 1936, Ruth Harkness met up briefly with a man thought to be Tangier Smith (but whom she referred to as Zoology Jones in later accounts) and refused his invitation to join forces with him. Instead, two expeditions soon converged on panda country. Among other frustrations, the Harkness party met with a strike by their coolies, leaving the party with no choice but to trundle their equipment through rough country in wheelbarrows. Even so, the Harkness expedition won the race (an amateur beating a professional) and returned to Shanghai with a still suckling female panda named Su Lin. Later, Tangier Smith was to claim that he had captured three pandas that year and that two had died on the journey out of China; implicit in this claim was the suggestion that Harkness had bought Su-Lin from him. The entire affair remains shrouded in mystery. Once back in America, Harkness was besieged by zoos seeking the honor of housing the panda, the two most serious contenders being the Bronx Zoo, and the Brookfield Zoo in Chicago. Eventually Chicago won out.

Meanwhile, Su-Lin had become the most famous animal of the century. So great was her effect on the public, which is easily captivated by a truly cute face, that the notion of shooting pandas for sport or for science almost immediately died out, the Roosevelt brothers saying that they would never do such a thing again. Other pandas were to come out of China both before and after the Second World War, and the panda remains to this day one of the most, if not the most, popular zoo animals in the world, eagerly sought after by zoo officials, as well as being the symbol of the World Wildlife Fund and a source of lasting inspiration to the toy industry.

Zoos — many of them, at least — were becoming big business, commanding huge audiences and millions of dollars in municipal, private and other funding. More than ever, zoo directors needed to be more than simply devoted animal people. To be successful they had to combine the wiles of a fundraiser and public-relations expert with the political and managerial energy of a city mayor. In many major zoos, they had to preside over not just the keepers and curators and veterinarians who saw to the well-being of the animal collection and the daily alarms and crises involved in that enterprise, but also growing bands of research scientists and programs, elaborate educational efforts, citizen support groups and volunteers, and the hordes that stream through the zoo each day — the public, with its needs for parking spaces, something to eat, souvenirs to buy and (increasingly in an age of growing concern about the welfare of animals) the reassurance that the exotic creatures they have come to see are "happy."

There is no completely successful analogy for a major zoo, but a comparison is often made with a city. Cities don't grow their own food, for example. It must all be transported in, and selected according to the tastes of the citizens. No city has as diverse tastes in food as does a zoo. Insectivores eat insects: a zoo may order 100 pounds (45 kg) of mealworms and 30,000 crickets each week. A typical week's order from the keeper of the Elephant House at the National Zoo (which includes hippos and giraffes) will include: four bags of oats, a bag of wheat bran, several bags of special diet pellets, numerous cans of vitamin and mineral supplements, many cases of evaporated milk and dried cereal, a case of honey, 50 pounds (22 kg) of potatos, 175 pounds (79 kg) of kale, three dozen eggs, 35 loaves of bread, 100 pounds (45 kg) of apples and 50 pounds (22 kg) of bananas. Four tigers and lions will consume fruit, vegetables, cereal, a dozen dead chicks, 200-odd pounds (90 kg) of special feline diet and nearly 500 pounds (225 kg) of meat. As zoo nutritionists learn more about the needs of the animals, special diets are developed; it is now possible to buy commercially, in cans just like at a supermarket, such specialties as Primate Diet and even Crane Diet.

As zoo management became more complicated, so too did the old triad of concerns — the animal's welfare, facilitating the keeper's job and providing pleasure to the viewer. A new form of zoo architecture had been developed at the turn of the twentieth century, created not by an architect but by an animal dealer, Carl Hagenbeck. His idea was simply to exhibit animals in a more naturalistic setting, and more or less at the visitor's eye level. He implemented these notions in his own private zoo in Stellingen, near Hamburg, in 1907. For the first time, zoo animals were exhibited in cages without bars: their enclosures were stage-like platforms separated from the public by impassable moats. The enclosures were landscaped with artificial rocks, plants and ponds. Most modern zoo exhibits that one sees today are imitations or modifications of Hagenbeck's original concept — especially in those zoos wealthy enough and possessed of sufficient territory to make the changeover. Taken to a happy extreme — where available space, sufficient funds and a proper climate permit, as in, for example, the San Diego Zoo — it is possible to create the semblance of an African veld, allow the animals virtually free run of the place, and confine the visitors to modified passenger trains. That solution is, of course, frequently impossible, but it is becoming clear through research done on both captive and wild animals that a large amount of space is not always necessary for the well-being of an animal. More important is the quality of the space.

Most animals cannot abide being totally surrounded by peering visitors. A proper enclosure will include a place where the animal can have privacy, to rest or to hide. The space between enclosure and visitor must be large enough so as not to violate the animal's flight distance — that is, the distance at which an animal will allow a human to approach before taking flight. In most instances, an exact replica of the animal's natural environment is not only impossible but unnecessary. Gibbons spend a great deal of the day swinging through trees, but a captive band of gibbons doesn't need an ersatz rain forest: it needs an environment with structural complexity comparable to tree branches. A construction of PVC pipe and a few resting platforms keeps gibbons active and largely fulfilled. Wild animals spend a good deal of the day foraging: in captivity, such activity ceases since dinner is supplied. But, without some compensating activity, many zoo animals are subject not only to obesity but to the debilitating stress of boredom. They can, and often have, grown extremely neurotic. Various kinds of indestructible toys are now common in zoo enclosures: empty beer kegs, milk jugs, jungle gyms, rubber buckets, used tires.

Not long ago it was common to see gorillas in sanitized, tiled cells, thought to be necessary to prevent disease. Wild animals, over generations, tend to build up a certain amount of immunity to the disease vectors common to their habitat. But, in a new habitat, such as a zoo, there are new diseases that can strike them down. The old-style enclosures tended to produce disease-free and pathetically unhappy zoo gorillas. New ape enclosures provide a relatively naturalistic habitat, with the floor covered with hay or leaves. The keepers will regularly sprinkle small food items, such as raisins, in the hay, and the gorillas spend hours each day contentedly and carefully sifting the substrate for treats. The result is active animals doing interesting and more natural things, which is good for both animals and visitors, but creates a lot more work for the keepers and requires greater vigilance and more frequent testing by veterinary staffs.

Another change that has taken place in this half of the century can be noticed in the same gorilla enclosure; namely, several animals in the same place, interacting. The tendency of zoos in the nineteenth and early twentieth centuries was to exhibit one or a pair of as many different species as they could obtain and fit into the available spaces. Today, zoo managers have realized that many species are social and thrive only in the company of their own kind. Many tamarins (small monkeys), for example, live their natural lives in extended families, with older offspring assisting parents in raising new babies. Without this early training, the tamarin is unequipped, in adulthood, to raise its own offspring. Thus, the trend since the 1960s has been for zoos to exhibit more individuals of fewer species. Animal welfare is put ahead, in this case, of visitor appetite.

For most tropical animals in cold-climate zoos indoor enclosures are essential. It has been found that such warm-weather creatures as bongo and other antelope can do perfectly well outdoors in winter temperatures as long as they have a heated place to rest: an open shed fitted with a few heat lamps is often sufficient. Other tropical species must stay indoors, but happily the cage with bars is on the way out. Often, thick laminated glass is enough to keep the animal in and it gives the viewer a clear look. Dark-colored, vertically strung wire is nearly invisible to the viewer and, in aviaries, provides an added dimension: the birds can be heard as well as seen. Some zoos are following the lead of the Bronx Zoo, in which bird habitats are lit while the passageway from which visitors view the birds is kept dark.

By the 1960s, it was increasingly clear that a "happy" animal in a zoo was one that was sufficiently at ease to breed. Increasing attention was given to this aspect of animal behavior. Led by the example of the London Zoo, several had arranged to purchase large tracts of land outside of cities, places where ungulates, in particular, could roam relatively freely and in herds, increasing the likelihood of breeding. Many zoos had added licensed veterinarians to their staffs, rather than relying on veterinary students, in an effort to keep the animals not only healthy but in good breeding condition. (It is worth noting that most veterinary training is geared to treatment of a handful of domestic animals — livestock and pets. But exotic animals are just that: exotic. What works for a cow may have virtually no effect on an eland, much less on a rhinoceros.)

A new era of wildlife conservation was in the offing. Most zoos had a strong commitment to this effort. The National Zoo, which is part of the larger Smithsonian Institution, began, in 1889 precisely, to conserve a remnant of the great herds of bison that had teemed across the plains of North America only decades before but that now were almost extinct. But the zoo's role in conservation was chiefly educational. It was hoped that visitors would experience the sight and smell and sound of real exotic animals, read the notice saying that this species is endangered and, with empathy heightened, go off and perhaps do something about it.

Then, in the late 1970s, the fears that many zoo people had harbored were confirmed by the Ralls studies. It was, perforce, a new day for zoos.

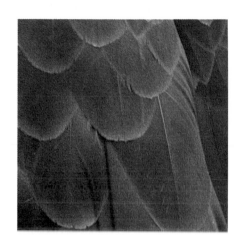

Animals of the Northern Region (Holarctic)

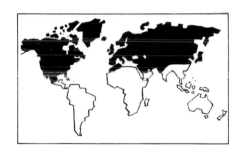

△ Zoos encounter all kinds of difficulties establishing conditions in which different species will breed. In the case of sable antelope (*Hippotragus niger*), not only is it useful to establish a herd, but in the experience of one zoo, individuals of the species also require privacy before they will mate.

▷ The alpine ibex (*Capra ibex ibex*) is a native of the mountainous regions of central Europe where the encroachments of humans have reduced its territory drastically. There are more than 250 of the animals in zoo collections worldwide. Most have been bred in captivity. The Assiniboine Park Zoo in Winnipeg has one of the larger breeding groups.

△ The beautiful white coat of the arctic wolf (*Canis lupus hudsonicus*) marks this specimen in the Metropolitan Toronto Zoo's densely-treed wolf exhibit.

◁ Although it has been persecuted by humans throughout much of its range in the Northern Hemisphere, the wolf (*Canis lupus*) is still fairly numerous in the wild. The largest member of the dog family, the wolf's unfortunate literary reputation causes many people to look on it with unwarranted dread.

△ The largest captive herds of the saiga antelope (*Saiga tatarica*) are in the USSR. The East Berlin Zoo, where this photograph was taken, also maintains a significant group.

▷ The aviaries for birds of prey at the Frankfurt Zoo house this bald eagle (*Haliaeetus leucephalus*), a bird whose dependence on fish and waterfowl that in recent years have been contaminated by DDT and other pollutants, has resulted in a seriously declining wild population.

◁ The alligator (*Alligator mississipiensis*) was once considered threatened, but is no longer on the list of endangered species. The Americas Pavilion at the Metropolitan Toronto Zoo contains a realistic simulation of the reptile's natural habitat.

◁ The giant panda (*Ailuropoda melanoleuca*) undoubtedly qualifies as an example of what Tom Foose, conservation coordinator of the AAZPA, has called "charismatic megafauna," that is, attractive, large animals that are capable of drawing large numbers of people into zoos. Pandas are in considerable danger in their natural habitat and, in addition, are difficult to breed in captivity. The Ueno Zoo in Tokyo has had some success using artificial insemination.

△ The Metropolitan Toronto Zoo is one of a few in North America to build exhibits that allow visitors to view polar bears (*Thalarctos maritimus*) both above and below the water. The New York Zoological Society's Central Park Zoo, Calgary Zoo and Chicago's Lincoln Park Zoo have comparable facilities.

▷▷ The polar bear (*Thalarctos maritimus*) is protected in the wild due to an agreement among five polar nations (Canada, Denmark, the United States, USSR and Norway) that forbids all but native peoples from killing them. It has long been a favorite among visitors to zoos, and generally adapts well to warmer climates. The bear shown is an inhabitant of the San Diego Zoo.

△ The wild boar (*Sus scrofa*), a native of central Europe, is reasonably well represented in European zoos.

▷ The range of the Rocky Mountain goat (*Oreamnos americanus*) extends from the mountains of Alaska to those of Montana and Idaho, but is now largely limited to the sanctuary provided by national parks in Canada and the United States. Not a true goat, but a goat-antelope, it is rarely seen in zoos.

According to an estimate made in 1988, there were about 800 Przewalski's horses (*Equus przewalskii*) worldwide. Some have been reintroduced into the wild in the Soviet Union, under controlled conditions, and a similar scheme is being mooted in China.

Like other large cats that lead relatively solitary lives and consequently require large territories in the wild, the cougar (*Felix concolor*) is increasingly threatened. The Metropolitan Toronto Zoo is home to this one.

Designated as vulnerable in the *Red Data Book*, the golden or snub-nosed monkey (*Rhinopithecus roxellanae*) is rarely seen outside of Chinese zoos. The Metropolitan Toronto Zoo had the loan of this pair from the People's Republic of China.

2 · By the Numbers

One of the starkest, most uncompromising zoological statements ever made was uttered in 1984 by a man named Ulysses S. Seal. He said that, "for a large segment of the life forms of this planet, evolution by natural selection has ceased."

Though he is employed at a veterans' medical center in Minnesota, Seal is a preeminent figure in the world of zoos by virtue of the fact that he became a fanatical record-keeper of zoo animal data. He was preceded by another outsider, an army man named Marvin Jones. Jones was fascinated by zoos and visited them wherever his extensive military travels took him. He began to keep genealogies of various zoo species around the world, for example, beginning what amounts to a studbook on golden lion tamarins, those perky zoo favorites native to the coastal rain forests of Brazil. After his military retirement, Jones went to work for the San Diego Zoo, and his efforts served as a kind of spiritual progenitor for Ulysses S. Seal's consuming interest. In 1977, Seal founded the International Species Inventory System, with a convenient acronym that hopefully invokes the ancient Egyptian goddess of fertility, Isis. ISIS, a project of the American Association of Zoological Parks and Aquariums (AAZPA), is now located in the Minnesota Zoo. It consists chiefly of a computer-maintained listing of individual animals in zoos, records of births and acquisitions from the wild. All told, ISIS tracks the genealogical data on 2,400 species in 326 zoos in 36 countries, as of 1989. It is essentially a social register of zoodom, with counterparts in Great Britain and Europe.

Leucopsar rothschildi, called variously Bali starling, Bali grackle and Bali mynah, is at the center of a project entered into by the Jersey Wildlife Preservation Trust and the government of Indonesia, the object of which is to return captive-bred specimens of this endangered species to the relative safety of a national park on its native island.

As much as anyone, Seal has the right to comment on the state of the animal kingdom. But what can he possibly mean by saying that, for many animals, natural selection is no longer operative? It has always been the engine of evolution, the sculptor of life as we understand it. How can it stop?

To understand what Seal meant and how zoos have responded requires a brief excursion into the science of genetics. A gene is essentially a set of instructions embodied in a vast manual of instructions called DNA, the long double-helical strand of amino acids that inhabits each cell. For the sake of simplicity, say there is a gene that instructs the growing organism as to size. Two large parents would, in most cases, pass along two size genes that say "large": let us call these size genes S. Two small parents would tend to produce small offspring, having passed along s genes. The offspring of two large parents could be called SS, those of small parents produce ss. Cross a large parent with a small one and you get Ss offspring. The size gene of the young of such parents contains two messages about size, and typically the S message masks the s message. Such a gene is called heterozygous, with a dominant S and a recessive s.

One needs only to look at the difference in size between a Pekingese and a mastiff to realize that, with enough mixing of parentage, there arises a great diversity from the mixture of such genes over many generations. The breeds share enough genes to be members of one species, but each individual is at least slightly different from any other. A dog breeder, obviously, can select for certain genes among parents to get bigger or smaller breeds.

In nature, each population of animals contains recessive and dominant genes, varying from individual to individual. And the mathematical possibilities are rendered all the more complex by the fact that genes can mutate or change, at random — for example, from the action of natural radiation on these delicate molecules — adding yet more genetic diversity to the population. Another way to think of this is: the organism as a piano concerto, each gene being a chord made up of several different notes. Generally speaking, the richer the chords, the better the concerto, and it is here that natural selection comes into play. In this musical analogy, natural selection can be thought of as the conductor on his podium in the concert hall (the environment) where each genetic concerto must be played. The conductor can vote yes or no at any moment. In nature, if a creature's unique genetic makeup is such that, if for any one of countless reasons, it does not survive in its environment long enough to reproduce, then its particular and unique genetic composition is gone forever from the larger pool of genetic compositions. Thus, the number of notes that are available to make up chords throughout the population at large is reduced — a countertendency (called "genetic drift") against the trend toward diversity. The less diversity in a given population, the less likely it is (or many of its members are) to thrive in a changed environment — and virtually any environment is subject to small or great change.

Among the species, extinct in the wild that have also died out in zoos, are thylacines or the Tasmanian wolf (top, pictured at the Hobart Zoo, Tasmania, about 1910), Syrian wild ass (center, believed to have breathed its last in the wild about 1930), and the quagga (the specimen shown in the London Zoo about 1872).

The Arabian oryx (*Oryx leucoryx*) — once extinct in its original range — is one of the endangered species singled out for special attention under the Species Survival Plan of the AAZPA. The largest breeding group outside of the Middle East has been established at San Diego Wild Animal Park.

In a small population, the tendency is for the homogenizing effects of genetic drift to outrun the diversifying effects of mutations, and a given chord tends to become reduced to one note (a recessive gene in this musical analogy), which, when too consistently expressed, is deleterious. The process is hastened by inbreeding, which tends to unmask recessive genes from both parents all the faster.

Such was the situation Ulysses S. Seal was describing. In short, for many species of animals and plants — especially the large ones — the reserves and parks set aside for them, as well as zoos, are too small to allow large enough populations for naturally occurring random mutations to keep up with genetic drift and inbreeding. In the larger sense, of course, natural selection will always continue to work, in such cases eventually selecting against a given species until it dies out altogether. This situation is called extinction, and it has happened countless times in the history of life. What Seal meant was that, unless mass extinctions are going to happen at a largely unprecedented rate and almost entirely because of the encroachment of mankind, then mankind has to step in and take over the selection process — in short, to play God.

No one is in any doubt that the ideal way to preserve wild species is to preserve large tracts of their habitat. Twenty-five percent of all species, at least, are presently threatened by loss of habitat. The situation is worse in areas of human poverty and political unrest, of course, where human needs take precedence. Drought and conflict in Africa's Sahel region has eliminated the scimitar-horned oryx from those precincts. Protracted conflict between Somalia and Ethiopia has almost surely extinguished the wild populations of Speke's gazelle. The loss of rain forests around the world is the most serious threat to wildlife since the Ice Ages, but it is not all a Third World problem. There are many who believe that even so vast an area as Yellowstone National Park is not big enough to support a viable grizzly bear population over very many more generations, and the wolves of Isle Royale in Lake Superior are apparently on the slope of an inevitable decline caused by lack of space.

Island ecologists have determined that the size of a place correlates directly to how many species can survive and how many will become extinct. All reserves and parks are of necessity "islands" too, surrounded by effective barriers of human habitation and land use. Just how large a park must be to maintain — naturally — its overall integrity is not known exactly, except in the case of a few predator species — typically the first to disappear from a reserve that is too small. The U.S. branch of the World Wildlife Fund (WWF), part of the Conservation Foundation, has embarked on a multidecade study in the Brazilian Amazon to shed light on this matter of minimum critical size. Taking advantage of a law that requires Amazon ranchers to leave half the rain forest intact when they clear jungle areas for cattle ranches, the WWF, in league with a Brazilian research organization, is isolating "islands" of rain forests of varying size — ranging from 25 to 250 acres (10 to 100 ha) — having first censused all the trees, animals and so on in the area. After the tract is isolated, periodic censusing will show how soon what species leave, eventually providing wildlife managers and planners with a series of formulas by which they can select areas for preservation and know how large a tract must be set aside to retain a given number of species. But, most of the answers from this study are a decade or more away; meanwhile, tropical rain forests around the world are being felled at a rate we can only guess at. One estimate is that forest areas equivalent to the State of Minnesota are lost each year. Imaginative and powerful international efforts are being made to slow down this rate of habitat destruction but, even in the best of prognoses, many species — especially large ones — will certainly be lost. A jaguar, for example, needs considerably more than a 24,700-acre (10,000 ha) area in the rain forest.

Conservation of such resources remains paramount but will inexorably be inadequate for many species. Enter the zoo, with its revolutionary new task: the active preservation of species, and of viable genetic diversity within species, against the day when habitats are restored and animals can be returned to them, or perhaps can merely be preserved in captivity — a kind of covenant humanity might well make with the Creator. Two millennia ago, in China, a riverine species of deer, called milou, was extinct in the wild and existed only in the mandarins' parks, which is where the French missionary Père Armand David saw them in the late nineteenth century. He shipped live specimens back to France, and Europeans (most notably the dukes of Bedford) maintained herds for about a century. Just recently, Père David's deer, as they came to be called, have been reintroduced to China. The persistence and power of such covenants need not be underestimated.

The need in the late 1970s was clear but many questions bloomed, most of them having to do with the question: how? A number of zoologists had anticipated this moment and among them was Michael Soule, then of the University of Michigan, now president of the Society for Conservation Biology. Soule reckoned that the human population, soon to be five billion, would quickly climb to ten billion and remain there for about 500 years before it began to decline (barring nuclear or other sort of catastrophe). During this demographic winter, there would be essentially no wilderness, virtually no land for wildlife reserves. Most large animals would have to be captive-bred in zoos against that day when a population decline allowed habitat to be reconstituted. Breeding such animals meant breeding for genetic diversity within the captive species not only to avoid the ills of inbreeding but also because no one knows what collection of genes works best for an animal in the wild. It was recognized that Johnny-One-Note species, genetically speaking, would soon fall prey to the grimmer side of natural selection once back in the wild — especially since no one can predict what the wild might be like in 500 years. Further, no one had sufficient hubris to think that a captive-bred population could achieve 100 percent of

All species of rhinoceros are endangered in the wild. There are approximately 700 white rhinoceros (*Ceratotherium simum*) in captivity, however, and it appears to adapt quite readily to a variety of conditions. The San Diego Wild Animal Park, shown here, provides a particularly appropriate setting.

the species' natural genetic diversity, so it seemed that 90 percent would be a reasonable goal.

Out of the esoterica of population genetics, a science that at the time was significantly absent from most zoos, there emerged a few key generalizations. A minimum of six "founders" could, if manipulated properly, produce a sufficient amount of genetic diversity in ensuing populations. Such manipulations would be, for example, making sure that the offspring of Founder Couple A bred only with the offspring of Founder Couples B and C. And the size of the population needed to maintain that diversity over time had much to do with the time between generations. Since any child is a product of the maternal and paternal genes (half from each parent), it follows that half of each parent's genes are lost in any given offspring. It works out mathematically that if the time between generations is short — as it is in mice — you need more in the population to maintain 90 percent of the original diversity over time. However, with an elephant, whose interval between generations is more like the human one, you need far fewer in what is called the "effective population." For example, with an animal with twenty-six years between generations, as in the case of some storks, the effective population needs to be only about forty — at least, mathematically. No group of animals is likely to understand this math and cooperate, however, so, practically speaking, the population needs to be four times that. For most species that would become candidates for such an effort, the required populations turned out to be fewer than 500. But, except for the likes of frogs and mice, no zoo has room for anywhere near 500 animals of a given species. Nor would anyone want all, or most, members of a species in one place lest they all fall prey to an epidemic or some other disaster.

Implacably, such numbers called for a high degree of cooperation among zoos, a new notion among these typically competitive institutions. For example, when the People's Republic of China determined to send two giant pandas to the United States as a gift to the American public, competition for the right to house them was stiff and bitter, and this was as recently as 1972. Eight years later, faced with the new math of zoodom, John Eisenberg of the National Zoo in Washington, D.C., summarized the situation at the annual meeting of the AAZPA: "No single zoo can, of itself, become a Noah's Ark."

The numbers also called for a new look in zoos — more individuals of fewer species — a kind of specialization. For the modern zoo, the days of the postage-stamp collection (one or two of everything) were over. It took courage for zoo managers to give up some crowd-pleasing variety so as to use more space for breeding populations. Most zoos and their directors are in the thrall of the local municipality, and much of their financing derives from public funds, awarded by politicians who are rarely zoological experts. Why, they might ask, get rid of a popular pair of giraffes, say, to make room for three more (boring) Eld's deer? The mayor of one U.S. city came close to firing the zoo director and his entire staff when he found they had shipped two popular gorillas elsewhere as part of a breeding effort. And even harder questions would be asked as zoos, with amazing celerity, moved into their new age.

The perpetuation of species would be accomplished by the seemingly cold computations of science, but policies in zoos have to be filtered down through curators to the ranks of zookeepers, the men and women who daily feed the animals, shovel out the excrement, and keep the senses tuned for any new smell or behavior that hints of trouble. The pay for a zookeeper is not typically overgenerous, and the hours are often inconvenient. It is not likely that zookeepers as a group have been analyzed as to motivation, educational background and other such parameters. Almost certainly zookeepers as a group are less well-understood than are the animals they tend. They are, purely and simply, animal people. While the science of exotic-reproduction biology has made extraordinary leaps in the last decade, it is usually the keepers, the animal people — those who can "read" their animals — who preside over successful breeders. There is a kind of magic to this, and zoo administrators know it.

In any event, in the 1970s, zoos had largely become net producers, rather than consumers, of exotic animals. In 1973, about 50 nations had signed a treaty restricting and, in some cases, totally banning international traffic in about 800 endangered species. By 1986, 90 percent of mammals and 75 percent of birds that were added to zoo collections had been bred in captivity. But, despite such success, there were problems.

A natural population of Siberian tigers, for example, will tend to have an equal number of males and females, with a larger proportion of adults, many newborns, fewer one-year-olds and even fewer two-year-olds, and so forth. This is a result of mortality among youthful tigers: few survive to adulthood. By 1973, successful breeding of

In some ways, the golden lion tamarin (*Leon topithecus rosalia*) is the prize example of the work of the modern zoo. With its habitat in the Brazilian rain forest reduced by an estimated 98 percent and its wild population down to a few hundred, the National Zoo in Washington coordinated a breeding project, subsequently joined by other zoos, that resulted ultimately in the return of some captive-bred animals to preserves established in the wild.

Siberian tigers had achieved a similar distribution of age and sex in American zoos. But, at that point, zoos achieved their carrying capacity for tigers, and breeding programs were curtailed. Within five years, there was only a handful of one-year-olds, no newborns, and an aging, almost entirely adult population. Ten more years and the whole tiger population in American zoos — infertile and geriatric — could have been lost. Another problem: of the 801 bird species bred in 1979, only 37 were considered endangered, rare or vulnerable, out of a list of 433 such species.

What is arguably the greatest single success story of an animal bred in captivity and returned to the wild is the golden lion tamarin. In fact, the effort to save this animal provided the model for all the breeding programs that followed. The ancestral home of these small golden-red monkeys is the coastal rain forests that stretch north from Rio de Janeiro. By the late 1960s, a mere 2 percent of the original forest remained. Perhaps some 600 of the tamarins hung on in isolated patches, and the world's zoos housed about 100, which rarely reproduced. A Brazilian scientist, Dr. Adelmar Coimbra-Cillio, raised the alarm, calling for the establishment of a Brazilian refuge and some cooperation among zoos, the first step of which was to accept no more wild-caught animals, thereby discouraging the animal trade, which was depleting the wild population at a great rate.

Within a year the zoo population was down to seventy. Studies in the wild and in zoos showed not only the extended-family arrangement necessary for the survival of these creatures but also that their diet in captivity was wrong. They needed more animal protein, such as from insects, and less fruit. With the help of the World Wildlife Fund (U.S.), a primate center was established near Rio and from there, and from Monkey Jungle in Florida, new insights accumulated, such as the fact that tamarins have personal preferences about whom they mate with, and that when females reach puberty, their jealous mothers push them out of the territory.

A formal international studbook was drawn up, to be orchestrated by the National Zoo in Washington. The plan called for a variety of research programs by zoos and universities and the collection into a handful of zoos of all the tamarins in captivity. The National Zoo constructed a new building for tamarins, but it was soon discovered that the stress of having other breeding groups of tamarins nearby caused less breeding activity: tamarin families were then separated and housed in distant buildings. They began to breed and grew heavier, averaging 26 ounces (750 g) as opposed to an earlier 21 ounces (600 g). Litters grew in size. By 1980, the population in zoos had doubled and, in no time, it would reach capacity: 400. By 1990, if unchecked, it would have reached 3,500. The managers of tamarins began to look to the wild, and there it was soon discovered that the wild tarmarins were even more inbred than the captive.

Brazilian scientists had managed to get a small preserve of rain forest set aside and, in 1983, two Americans from the National Zoo moved in to begin the job of restoring the forest, cutting fire breaks, studying wild tamarin behavior and educating Brazilian biology students in such techniques. A campaign began, as well, to educate local people about the plight of the tamarins. To the north, a band of captive tamarins was assembled in Washington and began to learn the lessons of living in the wild. They were taught to look for food that the keepers had hidden, and to land on soft, swaying branches. In 1984, the band of fourteen was taken to the Brazilian primate center for training and acclimatization and thence to the reserve.

The fourteen tamarins were released and slowly, over weeks, began to make themselves at home. By the middle of the next year, seven had succumbed — to predators mostly — but seven survived and, more important, had offspring. That year, 1985, two more bands were released, and others followed, some from European zoos. In some cases, the released animals have joined with wild tamarins, intermixing genetic material, and now there are several generations of tamarins born wild from originally captive founders. This was the first successful reintroduction of a primate to the wild.

Clearly, if zoos — with their growing ability to breed their own but with obvious limitations on space and funds — were to play an important role in the preservation of species, more than interzoo cooperation was called for. An overall strategy had to be agreed upon and coordinated centrally.

In North America, the logical center for any such planning was the American Association of Zoological Parks and Aquariums, itself located in Wheeling, West Virginia; however, the operator of ISIS was located at the Minnesota Zoo, a brand-new installation that had opened in 1978. Before long, the AAZPA announced the Species Survival Plan whereby more than thirty species were earmarked for special management (by 1989 the number was fifty). The main criterion, of course, for a species to be included was that it was imperiled in the wild, and even more so if it was the single representative of a genus or family. There had to be a record, or likelihood, of successful breeding in captivity. And there had to be a group of professionals at several zoos who had the time and resources to enter into a long-term management program. And utterly crucial was the existence of information — genealogical information, for it is only from such records, or studbooks, that a successful plan can be developed that will maximize genetic diversity within the species.

It takes time to develop the needed information, to maintain a studbook, and to work out the plan for a given species. Although not all of the fifty species designated as SSP species have complete plans worked out for them, typically the goal is much the same. Managers want to establish a population that is as diverse genetically as possible — preferably from ten to twenty founders; breed the population up to zoo carrying capacity; and spread the animals around, and then monitor the entire population, shipping animals back and forth as needed to avoid any further inbreeding. But strategies differ, depending on a host of factors, including population size, the age and number of founders and their relatedness.

For example, the St. Louis Zoo found itself faced with a nearly desperate situation — the Speke's gazelle, a native of the region of Ethiopia and Somalia and by then wiped out in the wild by war. The entire North American population consisted of fifteen badly inbred animals, all derived from one male and three females, a prime arena for the accumulated effects of inbreeding called an "inbreeding depression." The plan became a prototype of most Species Survival Plans. The only answer seemed to be to breed relentlessly the most severely inbred animals with each other, in the hopes of selecting for those genes that had enabled the animals to survive inbreeding so far, and to eliminate (through mortality) those recessive genes that led to inbreeding depression. This radical proposal seemed to work: the population soon doubled, and the young from the planned matings survived at a greater rate than those from previous matings. So, the Speke's gazelle appears to be saved from extinction, but the question remains: are the progeny truly Speke's gazelles? Thoughtful people disagree on the propriety of creating a "different" animal in order to save it, and zoo people often fret about the god-like role they must play, but play it they must.

The fifty species selected by the AAZPA for special treatment are:

INVERTEBRATE:
partula (a variety of snails) *Partula sp.*

AMPHIBIAN:
Puerto Rican crested toad *Peltophryne lemur*

REPTILES:
Chinese alligator *Alligator sinensis*
radiated tortoise *Goechelone radiata*
Aruba Island rattlesnake *Crotalus unicolor*
Dumeril's ground boa *Acrantophis dumerili*

BIRDS:
Humboldt penguin *Spheniscus humboldti*
Andean condor *Vulture gryphus*
California condor *Gymnogypa californianus*
hooded crane *Grus monacha*
red-crowned crane *Grus japonensis*
wattled crane *Bugeranus carunculatus*
white-naped crane *Grus vipio*
Guam rail *Rallus owstoni*
palm cockatoo *Probosciger aterrimus*
thick-billed parrot *Rynchopsitta p. pachyrhyncha*
Micronesian kingfisher *Halcyon cinnamomina*
Bali mynah *Leucospar rothschildi*

MAMMALS — PRIMATES
black lemur *Lemur macao*
ruffed lemur *Lemur variegatus*
golden lion tamarin *Leontopithecus rosalia*
lion-tailed macaque *Macaca silenus*
drill *Papio (Mandrillus) leucophaeus*
gorilla *Gorilla gorilla*
orangutan *Pongo pygameus*
bonobo *Pan paniscus*

MAMMALS — CARNIVORES
Asian small-clawed otter *Aonyx cinera*
maned wolf *Chrysocyon brachyurus*
red wolf *Canis rufus*
red panda *Ailurus fulgens*
spectacled bear *Tremarctos ornatus*
clouded leopard *Neofelis nebulosa*
snow leopard *Panthera uncia*
tiger *Panthera tigris*
Asian lion *Panthera leo persica*
cheetah *Acinonyx jubatus*

MAMMALS — HOOFED STOCK
Asian elephant *Elephas maximus*
Indian rhinoceros *Rhinoceros unicornis*
Sumatran rhinoceros *Dicerorhinus sumatrensis*
black rhinoceros *Diceros bicornis*
white rhinoceros *Ceratotherium simum*
Przewalski's horse *Equus przewalski*
Grevy's zebra *Equus grevyi*
Chacoan peccary *Catagonus wagneri*
barasingha *Cervus duvauceli*
okapi *Okapia johnstoni*
gaur *Boa gaurus*
addax *Addax nasomaculatus*
Arabian oryx *Oryx leucoryx*
scimitar horned oryx *Oryx dammah*

Among the most beautiful of cats, and among the most prized by the fur trade, the snow leopard (*Panthera urcia*) inhabits the highlands of central Asia where its prey is often scarce and where, in consequence, it requires a large territory in order to survive. Increasingly in competition with humans for space, its numbers are declining dangerously. It can be seen in about seventy zoos world-wide including, as shown, the Metropolitan Toronto Zoo.

One of the earliest Species Survival Plans was developed for the Siberian tiger and was soon matched by a European plan initiated by the International Union of Directors of Zoological Gardens, whose version of ISIS is located at the Institute of Zoology at the London Zoo. In all, 68 European zoos held 207 Bengal tigers in 1986, the results of 60 founders. Expectedly, the genes of these founders were variously distributed, some being overrepresented. The register at the Institute turned up 47 tigers that should not be allowed to breed

further. The plan calls for each female left in the breeding group to produce a litter at four to six years of age, and another at nine to eleven years. Females who are underrepresented are allowed to breed as often as they can. The plan also calls for shipping females around from zoo to zoo, always keeping the trips as short as possible to save money and for the animals' own well-being. In addition, there will be an exchange between European and North American zoos about every five years. By 1988, 100 Siberian tigers in North American zoos had changed residence at least once.

Siberian tigers breed easily in captivity, and it would seem that the species is one of the few large carnivores facing a secure future. Indeed, the Siberian tiger points up the difficulty of success. There is only so much room in zoos and only so much room for tigers. Thanks to good nutrition and health care, zoo animals tend to live longer than do their wild counterparts. And, as inbreeding is curtailed, there is less juvenile mortality. It doesn't take too many generations in such circumstances to produce an overpopulation, animals for which there is no room. There is a minimum population size based on genetic considerations and a maximum size determined by space. At some point a breeding animal's genes are no longer valuable — indeed, the reverse is true — in such managed populations. Males can be separated from females, and females can be implanted with contraceptive devices, but such manipulation is tricky and can skew the population toward older animals or to those already well-represented. What is to be done with surplus animals?

In all of North American zoos there is space for little more than 1,000 of the tiger/lion class of big cats. A proper population size for long-term genetic management is around 200, meaning that one-fifth of the space for such cats needs to be given over to Siberian tigers, leaving four-fifths for all the rest. By 1984, North American zoos were at capacity. At the Detroit Zoo, managers felt obliged to take the logical route of euthanasia for an old male Bengal, to make room for others who would contribute more salubriously to the tiger gene pool. Such a notion sounds outrageous to people unaware of, or unwilling to accept, the mathematical logic involved in genetic management, and the need to think in species, as opposed to individual, terms when a species is in peril. In Detroit, a public hue and cry led to an injunction against euthanizing the old male. Without public understanding of the need to make such awesome choices — or without huge injections of money to buy more space — Species Survival Plans will be severely impeded.

A handful of zoos have, over the years, been fortunate to acquire large blocks of land where exotic species can roam widely and more or less at will. Under these more natural conditions, breeding can improve dramatically, especially among animals that tend to be sociable by nature and live in groups or herds. The London Zoo maintains a large area, the Whipsnade Breeding Farm, out in the country. The New York Zoological Society operates its Rare Animal Survival Center on St. Catherine's Island, off the coast of Georgia.

In 1974, the U.S. government transferred land formerly used for agricultural research in Front Royal, Virginia, to the Smithsonian Institution for the National Zoo's conservation and research centers. The latter two centers are closed to the public, but there is many a skidmark on the roads near Front Royal, produced when people driving through the foothills of the Blue Ridge Mountains see a herd of scimitar-horned oryxes grazing on the side of a hill.

An adjunct to the San Diego Zoo is the San Diego Wild Animal Park where visitors can take a nearly hour-long train ride through open country and many different habitats, seeing animals in naturalistic settings. But this is also an important breeding farm as well; cheetahs did not breed in San Diego until they were moved from the main zoo to the park. Some forty white rhinos have been born there (white rhinos are sociable and need space to roam if they are to breed, while black rhinos tend to live in pairs and need less space). Przewalski's horse, Arabian oryx, and lowland gorilla are among the other animals bred in the park. There are more than 11 such off-exhibit breeding centers established by U.S. zoos for more than 100 species of mammals and birds and reptiles. Some private game farms and ranches also provided space for exotics. Britain's Whipsnade and Marwell Zoological Park both provide the same kind of facilities. One of the earliest such dedicated parks was Gerald Durrell's Jersey Wildlife Preservation Trust on the Channel island of Jersey, founded in 1959 as "a stationary ark" for breeding endangered species of animals in well-protected circumstances. Across the Channel, the zoos at Frankfurt, Basel and Zurich are important breeding centers.

Even so, it has been estimated that the 600-odd zoos in the entire world average a mere 55 acres (22 ha) in size, and all of them would fit into Brooklyn, one of New York City's five boroughs. Space, then, is at a premium. Noah's 90-cubit ark (a cubit being the length of an arm from elbow to fingertip) seems, in retrospect, a bit small to save all the creatures from the Flood. And so does 35,000 acres (14,000 ha), especially in light of the fact that there are some 2,000 bird and mammal species alone that could benefit from SSPs.

In a few rare instances, suitable habitat is available back in the wild, and one of the goals of the overall Species Survival Plan is precisely that: to put captive-bred animals back in the wild whenever possible. Twenty years ago, there were no wild Arabian oryx in Oman and only a handful elsewhere on the Arabian peninsula. This fleet, sandy-colored creature had been hunted to near nonexistence almost overnight, succumbing to automatic weapons and vehicles that could match its speed. Such high-tech hunting had already eliminated the Arabian race of the African ostrich. In 1962, a London preservation group, with grants from the World Wildlife Fund and the Skikar Safari Club, rounded up three of the remaining few wild oryx. These animals, with others that were donated by the rulers of Saudi Arabia and Kuwait, and the London Zoo, formed the nucleus of the World Herd of Arabian Oryx. By 1969, there were a reported 200 of these animals left in the wild, and none was reported after

London Zoo's first Przewalski's horses took up residence at the turn of the century.

1972. By the end of 1980, a dozen zoos around the world housed 400 Arabian oryxes, and a year later 10 were chosen from Phoenix and San Diego to be returned to Oman. There, under the protection of the Sultan of Oman, they have thrived and multiplied. Two years later, some 30 animals were released into a Jordanian reserve.

In a similar fashion, British zoos have brought the scimitar-horned oryx back to a reserve in Tunisia and Père David's deer to two Chinese reserves, one near Shanghai and one near Beijing. The original population of 59 reintroduced animals has passed 100, and the Chinese intend to use this stock to replenish other habitats.

Attempts at reintroduction are under way for a few species of birds as well. The Guam rail, for example, was wiped out by an egg-eating snake introduced to the island during the Second World War. Plans are afoot to release captive-bred birds, not to Guam where the snake seems ineradicable, but to a nearby island where the habitat appears comparable. But returning birds to the wild can be tricky — in part because scientists may not really know what components of the birds' original habitat are essential. Some 3,000 Hawaiian geese — the nene — have been released into their "native" habitat — the volcanic highlands — over the past few decades. But most pairs do not breed every year, and when they do they rarely manage to raise the goslings to adulthood. Why? No one knows, but recently paleontologists have found the fossil remains of the nene and a number of long-extinct geese and goose-like ducks in the lowlands. Perhaps, when these other birds were driven toward extinction by the arrival of humans, the nene was able to establish a marginal existence higher up — an existence that perhaps would have been shortened in any event because of a scarcity of food.

The Jersey Wildlife Preservation Trust is attempting to return the pink pigeon to the island of Mauritius. The birds have been released in a large botanical garden (not their ancestral home) so they can be more carefully observed after release, but there have been a number of problems. If the wind is blowing when they are released, the birds get confused and, worse, get lost. There are egg predators, even in a botanical garden, including Indian mynahs, and small boys. New plans call for releasing the birds far away from people.

The Jersey Trust is one of four organizations that have linked up to reintroduce to the island of Bali its only endemic vertebrate (that is, the only vertebrate that evolved there and nowhere else) — the small white Rothschild's mynah. The others in the consortium are the AAZPA, the Indonesian government, and the International Council of Bird Preservation. Some 40 of the birds were taken, mostly from American zoos, to the Surabaya Zoo for training and acclimatization. The wild population at the time was reported to be a mere 200, all in an area called Bali Barat, which has only recently been made a national park. The plan is to release some 500 birds in the wild by the early 1990s. All told, there are about 500 birds in zoos at this time, but many of them come from a very few founders and they breed only uncertainly. To avoid inbreeding and to arrange compatible pairs, Rothschild's mynahs are being moved around in Great Britain and North America at an astonishing rate. A curator at the Bristol Zoo, for example, received a polite suggestion in 1988 from Georgina Mace at the London Zoo's Institute of Zoology to ship mynah number 382 to Harewood Bird Garden in Yorkshire and to expect a male, number 256, to arrive soon, to mate with female number 381. Further, it would be best if the Bristol people could send number 636 to London for sexing. And so it goes. The zoos don't have to comply, of course, but, it has been the rare occasion when a reputable zoo has failed to go along with this kind of matchmaking. They are inhabited by animal people, after all.

Captive breeding of birds is tricky but a major success has been achieved with the lammergeier or bearded vulture, a huge bird with a nearly nine-foot (3 m) wingspan that formerly was a common scavenger in the Pyrenees and the Alps. Thought to be more of a predator — on chamois, sheep and even children — than a scavenger, it was nearly eliminated altogether, but a reintroduction program got underway at the Austrian Alpine Zoo in Innsbruck. Managers there took advantage of the bearded vulture's habits, one of which is for the older chick in the nest usually to kill its younger sibling. So, younger chicks are removed and reared by hand, and the two are reunited once the age of aggression is past. Then both will be placed on a ledge and formally released. For a time, food is dropped onto the ledge (the dropping-off unobserved by the beneficiaries to insure that the birds don't associate food with people), and gradually they learn to fend for themselves. As of 1988, 12 birds out of 13 had survived, released near Salzburg, and were plying the mountains into Switzerland and Italy. The program looks toward fifteen years of releases from the same spot, relying on the birds to establish their own scavenging grounds. Unlike the California condor, a late Pleistocene holdover whose large mammal food has become extinct, the lammergeier has a main source, the chamois, that still exists plentifully in the Alps and, often caught in avalanches, becomes frozen and pops up from the snow, as one commentator said, "like out of an icebox."

There are many points of view, even philosophies, in wildlife management and conservation. Some observers feel that putting time and energy and resources into saving a few species in zoos distracts people from the need to save habitat. The release of the golden lion tamarins suggests another point of view. The people engaged in the release mounted a local educational campaign about the plight of the animal and the nature of their program. The tamarin became a popular local cause, even a symbol, and before long helped vitalize conservation movements nationally. Since the first band was released, the Brazilian government has been moved to place several more tracts of coastal rain forest under protection. Habitat thus has been saved in this instance, thanks to a reintroduction of an endangered animal — habitat not only for the tamarins but, willy-nilly, for the maned sloth and hundreds of other creatures.

Animals of Africa and Arabia (Ethiopian)

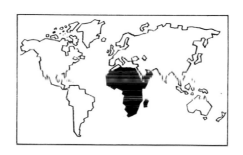

△△ Among the most popular of zoo animals, some long-lived individual gorillas (*Gorilla gorilla*) have become famous, notably Guy, who was a fixture at the London Zoo for thirty-one years, and Massa who was nearly fifty when he died at the Philadelphia Zoo. The albino gorilla at the Barcelona Zoo, Snowflake, also has many fans among zoo-goers.

◁◁ The lowland gorilla (*Gorilla gorilla*), and the related mountain gorilla, whose gentle disposition and vegetarian habits were described in books and on film by the naturalist Dian Fossey, are increasingly endangered in their native Africa. There may be, at most, 50,000 left, but poachers and steady encroachments on habitat are reducing their number. The Metropolitan Toronto Zoo (shown) is one of many working to establish a stable captive-bred population.

The Metropolitan Toronto Zoo has enjoyed fair success breeding the damara zebra (*Equus burchelli antiquorum*), a species of zebra not yet considered to be endangered. Like other ungulates that browse on African grasslands, however, the zebra is increasingly in competition with humans who would put the land to agricultural use.

The vulturine guinea fowl (*Acryllium vulvurinum*) is the largest of the guinea fowl family. Native to Africa, it appears to have the capacity to survive in a very dry environment. It has done well in San Diego Zoo and Toronto Zoo, in both of which several generations have been reared.

△
◁ The studbook for Somali wild ass (*Equus africanis somaliensis*) is presently held at the East Berlin Zoo. Other zoos keeping the animal include Basel's, where this pleasant treed and watered paddock is maintained.

△ Largest of the true gazelles, the Addra gazelle (*Gazella dama ruficollis*) is closely related to the Mhorr, red-necked and dama gazelles. All are native to the arid northern regions of Africa where, however, they are severely threatened. They adapt readily to the desert climate of California, as here in San Diego.

▷ Although it is protected in the wild, the African bush elephant (*Loxodonta africana*) is nevertheless in decline because of the human appetite for ivory and its own appetite for vegetation which frequently places it in competition with humans.

◁ The young of addra gazelles (*Gazella dama ruficollis*) are usually separated from the herd before they are six months old lest they be set upon by the older animals.

◁ The sitatunga (*Tragelaphus spekei*) has been bred in substantial numbers in captivity. The group shown is in the Bronx Zoo. The New York Zoological Society maintains a larger group in the Survival Center in Georgia.

△ The sacred ibis (*Threskiornis aethiopica*), with its long, down-turned beak and black-tipped wings, appears regularly in the hieroglyphics of the ancient Egyptians. It remains a common bird in marshy areas throughout Africa.

△ The sacred or hamadryas baboon (*Papio hamadryas*) was revered by the ancient Egyptians. Like many primates, it is sociable, and does best in a group dominated by a single male. It is quite common in zoos — in this case, the Berlin Zoological Gardens.

◁ A severely endangered species in the west African rain forest, the mandrill (*Papio sphinx*) is a favorite of visitors to zoos. Toronto maintains an extended family troop of them, as does Barcelona Zoo, one of whose specimens is shown.

▷ The snow leopard (*Panthera urcia*) is gravely endangered in its native highlands in India, China and the Soviet Union. According to one estimate, the wild population is no more than 500. There are about 300 in captivity.

The grey-necked crowned crane (*Balearica regulorum*) is found in many parts of Africa, but is threatened both by hunting and the systematic draining of the wetlands that provide its home. Frankfurt Zoo and Jersey Wildlife Preservation Trust are among the zoos keeping captive specimens.

The black rhinoceros (*Diceros bicornis*) is the subject of major campaigns by World Conservation International, the Zoological Society of London and the World Wildlife fund, to track and enumerate the remaining specimens in the wild and to establish refuges for them in Africa. About half the specimens kept in zoos worldwide were born in captivity.

◁ The South African oryx or gemsbok (*Oryx gazella gazella*), a strikingly marked antelope whose horns are some three feet (1 m) long, is not yet scarce in the wild. The Metropolitan Toronto Zoo, among others, is experiencing some success in building a viable breeding group.

△ The okapi (*Okapia johnstoni*), a distant relative of the giraffe, had not been seen by any Caucasian before the present century. The first to reach Europe were sent from central Africa to the Basel Zoo in 1949. (Of ten that embarked on the voyage, only two arrived alive at the zoo.) This individual, in the San Diego Wild Animal Park, is one of about seventy in captivity.

◁ The London Zoo has several reticulated giraffes (*Giraffa camelopardalis
reticulata*) in Regent's Park and more at
Whipsnade. In London they are
housed with other hoofed stock in
this venerable brick building near the
Regent's Canal.

▷ In the Metropolitan Toronto Zoo the
Masai giraffes (*Giraffa camelopardalis
tippelskirchi*) are free to roam in a large,
treed paddock.

△ The smaller African antelope, including Kirk's dik-dik (*Madoqua kirki*), tend to be nervous and retiring. Consequently, they are a good deal more difficult to breed in captivity than their larger relatives. A number of American zoos are attempting to raise them including Dallas, Philadelphia, San Antonio and the National Zoological Park in Washington.

▷ Only its Asian cousin is considered to be endangered, but the lion (*Panthera leo*) is one of the handful of animals that can scarcely be omitted from any zoo collection. It breeds with relative ease, and it is not unusual for a captive female to be implanted with a contraceptive device to prevent overcrowding in the limited space that zoos can provide.

◁ The dominant male of a group of red or Patas monkeys (*Erythrocebus patas*) is often too preoccupied guarding his extended family from the possible encroachment of competing males to take any part in their daily round of exploration and play.

Δ The caracal (*Felix caracal*), a lynx found in Africa and India, is not presently considered to be threatened in the wild. Toronto is one of a number of zoos with caracals in its collection.

◁ The ostrich (*Struthio camelus*) is an inhabitant of most zoos, and not yet considered to be endangered in the wild. It can be an aggressive and dangerous animal, capable of inflicting serious wounds with its kick when attacking to protect its territory.

▷ The ring-tailed lemur (*Lemur catta*), one of a number of species unique to the island of Madagascar, is the recipient of particular attention at the Jersey Zoo, where a significant breeding group has been established.

▷▷ The shoebill or hammerhead stork (*Scopus umbretta*) lives in African marshes and swamps where it eats lungfish, watersnakes, young turtles and even crocodiles. Recent estimates of the wild population put it at about 11,000 and declining. It has never been bred successfully in captivity although Frankfurt Zoo, where this picture was taken, and others including Chicago's Brookfield Zoo, continue to try.

◁ About sixty percent of all land vertebrates are creatures of the night. More and more zoos are therefore showing such nocturnal mammals as the fennec fox (*Fennecus zerdu*) in exhibits that use red light and other techniques to reverse night and day. Grzimek House in the Frankfurt Zoo, named after the director who rebuilt the zoo in the aftermath of the Second World War, is one example among many of such a facility.

◁ Breeding herds of Kordofan or Addra gazelle (*Gazelle dama ruficollis*) have been established in a number of American zoos that have the space to recreate something like the savannah in which the species originated. This includes San Diego Wild Animal Park, the New York Zoological Society's Rare Animal Survival Center on St. Catherine's Island in Georgia (which is not open to the public) and the San Antonio Zoo, Texas.

▷ A significant group of common waterbuck (*Kobus ellipsipyrmnus*) is maintained by the Zoological Society of London at Whipsnade. Other groups can be seen at Oklahoma City Zoo where hoofed stock is a specialty, San Diego Wild Animal Park and the Limburgse Zoo in Genk, Belgium.

△ The hippopotamus (*Hippopotamus amphibius*) is extinct in some of its original range in Africa, but still relatively numerous in other areas. Because its meat is not fatty and is as palatable as that of cattle and pigs, attempts have been made to utilize it for human nourishment. In the background, at the Basel Zoo, is a white-faced whistling duck.

▷ About one quarter of the world's captive stock of the delicate African klipspringer (*Oreotragus oreotragus*) are kept at the Frankfurt Zoo where a breeding program has been in place for a number of years. Zoo staff are careful to keep groups of the antelope in separate enclosures, both to control breeding and as a defence against the damage that might be wrought by infection or disease.

3 · High-Tech Conservation

In 1984, there were a number of bizarre, headline-making births in zoos in America and Great Britain — the result of embryo transplants. In May, a quarter horse named Kelly in the Louisville Zoo in Tennessee made history when she gave birth to a zebra. Two weeks later, in the Cincinnati Zoo, a common African antelope, an eland, gave birth to a bongo, a much rarer antelope valued at $25,000 apiece. The infant zebra was the first ever born to a horse, the bongo was the first successful embryo transplant between two genera. Any such intervention as an embryo transplant is dangerous to the mother; to intervene in a more common animal like an eland or a horse is thus safer overall, if it can be made to work. The Bronx Zoo in New York had already implanted the embryo of a gaur, the world's largest cattle and an endangered species from India, into Flossie, a Holstein cow, via surgery, but the Cincinnati Zoo proclaimed its bongo the first nonsurgical "transcontinental exotic embryo transfer." The bongo embryos had been brought from the Los Angeles Zoo to Cincinnati via commercial airline, taped to the body of the Cincinnati researcher.

Meanwhile the London Zoo had implanted both zebra and Przewalski's horse embryos in horses at an equine fertility unit near Cambridge and, while the zebra aborted late in pregnancy, a Przewalski colt, named Tarot, was born in June. Later, in September, the London Zoo announced the birth of the first frozen embryo

Wild herds of Przewalski's horse (*Equus przewalski*) still roamed the Mongolian plains as recently as the 1940s, but as urban civilization expanded, the animal fled to land less capable of sustaining it. By the 1960s it had vanished from its original range. It survives only in zoos and parks.

transfer — two baby marmosets whose embryos had been frozen for a week before being implanted. Six weeks later, the Cincinnati Zoo claimed a first in the frozen-exotic business when an eland gave birth to a baby eland. This baby had been removed from its mother as a seven-day-old embryo, had been frozen in liquid nitrogen for a year and a half, then thawed and implanted. Thus, it was born twenty-seven, not nine, months after conception. Cincinnati could claim that though their frozen embryo emerged after London's marmosets, it had been frozen first, and implanted first.

As the new age of cooperation swept the world of zoos, there arose briefly an odd, even unseemly, form of competition: the desire for a new category of "firsts." For years, biomedical researchers had used laboratory animals and others to develop techniques for assisting the human reproductive process, as had researchers used these techniques in the livestock industry. For humans it was a matter of helping couples have a child; for livestock it was a matter of increasing by leaps and bounds the contribution of particularly desirable animals to the gene pool. By the 1970s, a considerable panoply of means to sidestep reproductive difficulties or to speed up the process were available — fertility drugs, artificial insemination (AI), embryo transplants, *in vitro* fertilization (that is, test-tube babies). Much of this had become fairly routine. But in the 1980s, efforts began in earnest to take what had been learned from animals for the benefit of mankind and use it for the benefit of wildlife and exotic animals in captivity.

There would be many firsts in this brave new world but soon activity settled down to the arduous and time-consuming business of accomplishing systematic science rather than spectacular feats. It was no accident that most of these early embryo transfers had been accomplished with near-relatives of domestic animals because that is where the expertise and the techniques were to be found. Frosty, the first frozen dairy cow, had been born in the early 1970s. The notion of preserving the germ plasm of every endangered species against the time when there was room again for wildlife in the wild — the frozen zoo — had emerged not long after Frosty, but early attempts at even so common a practice as artificial insemination pointed up the difficulties involved in working with exotics. Species differ from one another not just in taxonomic texts, but in reality: they are biochemically different. Even closely related species can be strikingly different. Zoo researchers have found the blood levels of particular hormones necessary for successful reproduction vary widely among members of the cat family. What might work to inseminate a snow leopard may be way off the mark for a cheetah.

Meanwhile, semen that has been collected for AI must be maintained in a culture medium and at a certain temperature, or frozen. If it is to be used within a few hours, the semen of bulls and rams should be kept at 86°F (30°C), but it turns out that semen from such species as elephants and tigers must be kept at room temperature (70°F [21°C]). Very few of these details were known at the time.

In any event, the headline births in zoos in 1984 served to point out the value inherent in the techniques of artificial reproduction (and, as headlines do, they increased public awareness of the problems of wildlife). With the geneticists and studbook keepers ordering animals about the landscape in the name of genetic diversity, there is a considerable risk. It is dangerous to move an animal, and costly. The $25,000 bongo is a sturdy animal but fragile when thrust into a box and put aboard an airplane. The logistical aspects of SSPs would be well-served if one could carry what amounts to an entire potential herd of bongos on one's person in an airline passenger's seat. Also, zoo animals often carry with them diseases that would be dangerous to domestic livestock, a problem that could be lessened by importing germ plasm, rather than whole animals. And, of course, securing germ plasm from the field and using it to enrich the captive gene pool (and in some cases vice versa) makes sense in global matchmaking.

Any zoo manager will tell you that by far the best way to conserve wildlife is to conserve its habitat, and that captive breeding per se is an emergency measure. Similarly, almost anyone involved in the high-tech world of artificial breeding will tell you that it is always best if a captive pair will mate freely. Many species will breed easily in captivity — Siberian tigers, African lions, Guam rails, to name a few. But many species do not breed so well in such conditions — clouded leopards or Guam kingfishers, for example. Gorillas are subtle and complicated: sometimes two gorillas simply don't like each other, and there can be further behavioral complications. The zoo in Melbourne, Australia, found itself with a pair of gorillas, which, though unrelated, had grown up together since infancy. Evidently they thought of each other as siblings and thus would not mate. Zoo officials artificially inseminated the female and, in June 1984, she gave birth to a baby male, the first product of AI in gorillas to survive. The mother would have nothing to do with the offspring, however, and it had to be hand-reared. One can rarely tell what will happen from such interventions in nature — at least, not without a great deal of research and experience. It has been found that clouded leopards simply will not mate unless the pair has been brought up together since infancy (the opposite of gorillas). Of course, this presents a significant obstacle to the kind of genetic management of matings that is called for, and points to the value of artificial techniques.

AI was employed in 1984 in the attempts to get the two giant pandas in Washington to produce offspring. The two had mated but observers felt that the male, Hsing-Hsing, had performed in a substandard way. Hastily (the breeding season for pandas lasts only a few days), semen from the London Zoo's panda, Chia-Chia, was flown in, and Ling-Ling was impregnated. Subsequently she gave birth to a live cub, which unfortunately died of a respiratory ailment. Analyses proved that the cub had been sired by the maligned Hsing-Hsing.

AI, of course, first involves collecting semen from males; typically, this is done while the animal is anesthetized by applying a very mild and harmless electric shock. In many zoos it has become routine to collect semen whenever the animal, for one reason or another, is anesthetized. Anesthetization itself is risky, though far less so today thanks to the efforts of zoo veterinarians to work out precise dosages and other protocols for individual species. However, the stress created in such intervention can interfere with the reproductive process, affecting the viability of the semen, and the act of storing it in a freezer can produce ill-effects, varying species by species, and presumably individual by individual. By the late 1980s, however, scientists at the National Zoo in Washington had worked out enough of these details to suggest that a frozen-sperm bank for about a dozen ungulate species was a practical short-term goal.

So far, successful AI has taken place among some mammals and birds. Reptiles have proven more difficult: researchers at the London Zoo, for example, have reported numerous failures to discover a technique for collecting semen from snakes.

Nevertheless, any such intervention brings with it its own risks that must be weighed. And, of course, there is the female to be considered. All the frozen semen in the world is of no practical value unless there is sufficient understanding of the subtleties of the female's reproductive physiology and schedule. This too varies species by species. A case in point is the black-footed ferret, the most endangered of North American mammals. These ferrets lived in association with (and preyed upon) the "towns" of prairie dogs that were formerly common throughout the arid American west but had been regularly eradicated as "varmints" by people engaged in agriculture. By the mid-1980s, the last black-footed ferrets were eking out a living in Wyoming when a plague struck the prairie dogs, eliminating the ferrets' chief sustenance. To make matters worse, distemper struck the ferrets and, by 1986, it was reckoned that there were twenty-one ferrets left, six of them already in captivity. The U.S. Fish and Wildlife Service decided that the only course was to bring all the wild ones in and breed them in captivity. That department alerted three western universities and the National Zoo to prepare plans for a captive-breeding program.

Practically nothing was known about the reproductive physiology of these animals and, against the possibility that the captives would not breed successfully on their own and mindful of the need to breed them up in population size rapidly, the National Zoo began a program of research that took two years, using what seemed to be a viable substitute, the closely related European ferret. Eventually zoo researchers were able to produce several litters composing in all thirty-one European ferrets, using AI, and in the bargain successfully freeze ferret semen, providing guidelines that can be presumed to be safe for the black-footed ferret. Essentially the process consists of freezing semen — mixed with egg yolk as a protein-rich extender providing nutrients and bulk — in pellets on blocks of dry ice. The

In its home, in the remnants of India's rain forest, the wild population of the lion-tailed macaque or wanderoo (*Macaca silenus*) has been reduced to a beleaguered vestige. Captive breeding groups have been established in many zoos, from Dublin to Winnipeg. The National Zoological Park in Washington and San Diego Wild Animal Park have enjoyed notable successes with this species.

pellets are then stored in canisters of liquid nitrogen at a bone-chilling -385°F (-196°C). Semen from the domestic ferrets was frozen for eighteen months before it was thawed and used for AI. So, high-tech methods may bring this little predator back from the brink. Other notable successes in exotic AI have occurred at the London Zoo, which, for example, achieved five live births from blackbuck antelopes in 1986 out of a mere nine tries.

Even more complex is the series of steps involved in embryo transplants. Typically the donor female is given an array of hormones that cause her to superovulate, producing maybe thirty more eggs than she would normally. This is akin to double-clutching birds. In many bird species that typically have only one clutch of eggs, if these eggs are removed, the female will produce a second clutch. This phenomenon has been taken advantage of widely to propagate rare birds more quickly, as in the case of the California condor, all of which are now being bred in captivity in San Diego and Los Angeles.

In any event, say the plan is to collect embryos from a rare Eld's deer and implant at least some of them into common white-tailed deer, which are to act as surrogate mothers. Once the hormone-treated Eld's deer has begun to produce eggs, she is impregnated, usually artificially. Meanwhile, unless the embryos are to be frozen for later use, the white-tailed surrogates have to be standing by, ready to receive them, and this usually entails giving them prostaglandins or other hormones that will start their reproductive cycle at the right moment.

After a period of days, the Eld's deer's embryos leave the mother's ovaries and travel down the uterus where, in due course, they become implanted in the uterine wall. The trick is to intervene before the implantation takes place and find them (they are about the size of the dot over an i, or smaller). Once located, they are flushed out and examined microscopically. Only those that appear to be the healthiest are then implanted in the surrogates. Choosing the right moment to intervene — that is, after ovulation but before implantation in the wall of the uterus — depends on what species one is working with, and much of this process simply had to be discovered by trial and error.

Another technique, developed for humans, is *in vitro* fertilization, the production of so-called test-tube babies. This process involves flushing out the eggs, as above, and fertilizing them in a dish for transplanting either into the original mother or into a surrogate. If something goes wrong with an AI or embryo-transplant procedure and it doesn't work, there is little way of finding out why. With *in vitro* fertilization, however, scientists can observe and study the crucial process of fertilization and the animal's reproductive competence. In 1987, after two years of work, the National Zoo announced the first birth of a carnivore by this means — three litters of domestic cats. The following year, the Cincinnati Zoo announced the birth of an Indian desert cat from a surrogate domestic cat.

So, by the end of the 1980s, zoos found themselves with several useful new arrows in their quiver, the early development of species-by-species techniques for making last-ditch stands, for further enabling the speedy compliance with the suggestions and directions of the geneticists. And these match-making decisions could be made with ever-increasing precision, thanks to yet other technologies.

Even a good studbook — all of them being relatively new items — contains some question marks. If the founders of a zoo population included a number of animals caught in the wild, for example, one might question how closely or distantly related they were. A technique called electrophoresis can help supply answers. Electrophoresis consists of taking a blood sample, putting it into a gel and passing that through an electric field. The procedure causes certain proteins in the blood to move a certain distance, and these distances can be interpreted in a manner similar to that used with supermarket bar codes. The closer in pattern two samples are to each other, the more closely the animals are related. This is a relatively "soft" method, in the sense that one could question whether the proteins thus measured actually and precisely represent the whole story genetically. It was useful when no other tool was available to extract such genetic information.

Then, in the mid-1980s, along came the ultimate tool: DNA fingerprinting. This process quickly triggered a revolution in molecular genetics, and has found its way into the courtroom because it provides one with the ability to link, without any doubt at all, such a small piece of evidence as a hair or a bit of semen to an accused murderer or rapist. Something akin to electrophoresis, it consists of cutting particular sequences of DNA into separate pieces and labeling them. The pieces, in turn, are put into a gel that sorts them by size — resulting ultimately in a black-and-white representation of an animal's genetic code, again rather like a bar code.

The technique is especially valuable in such situations as the California condor where, of twenty-eight individuals in captivity, only half have known parents. At the same time they must all be related to some degree, and DNA fingerprinting has established which specimen is farthest from which genetically, a boon to breeding strategy. The San Diego Zoo is fingerprinting its Galápagos tortoises, which are all descended from dwellers of the Galápagos Islands, though until now there has been no way to tell which islands. Since the tortoises have at least recently evolved in relatively isolated island populations, it would seem reasonable to try to reflect those differences in breeding captive ones. For, while there is always the danger of an inbreeding depression, there is also something called an "outbreeding depression."

For example, among African elephants there are two major subspecies — the savannah and the forest — and at the extremes these can be identified by the density of their tusks and the size of their ears. But there are intermediate groups as well, which have diverged in subtle ways in the evolutionary process. To force these divergent

The Galapagos tortoise (*Testudo elephantopus*) is not quick, but is surprisingly powerful. Desmond Morris, sometime curator of mammals at the London Zoo, and before that, presenter of a television program about zoos in Great Britain, once watched a tortoise bulldoze its way out of a wooden corral and proceed to topple cameras and scatter their crews in its determination to avoid a television appearance.

types to breed can lead to an outbreeding depression — or even just a great deal of dangerous trouble in the typically hard-to-manage matings of captive elephants. Researchers at the St. Louis Zoo are working on a technique to use DNA fingerprinting to differentiate these subgroups, based on analysis of a small piece of tusk, so that elephant breeders can better steer this course between Scylla and Charybdis.

This research could have interesting side-effects in the wild as well. Several African nations that no longer have wild elephant populations retain elephant-exporting quotas and are often used as conduits for elephant ivory poached from other countries. It may become possible for customs people to identify rapidly just where a piece of ivory came from by DNA fingerprinting and thus gain another tool for discouraging this sorry trade.

Yet another application of these high-tech tools to the wild is among Akbar's nemesis — cheetahs. In some game parks, cheetahs suffer from a rate of infant mortality as high as 70 percent. Captive breeding, though counting a few successes, has been comparatively ineffective. One of the most successful such programs was established in 1971 by the National Zoo of South Africa, near Pretoria. Even there, however, success rates were low, and in 1981 the director invited researchers from the National Zoo in Washington to take a look.

The three researchers were well aware that low fecundity and high infant mortality were signs of inbreeding. Even so, they were stunned to find that cheetah sperm concentrations were only about 10 percent of those of domestic cats, and that some 70 percent of sperm were deformed. (In a bull a mere 20 percent deformity means, for all intents and purposes, that the bull is sterile.) The researchers also collected blood samples and analyzed them. What emerged was an astonishing picture of one of the most inbred wild-animal populations ever discovered. The fifty animals studied were virtually identical genetically. They demonstrated less genetic variability than do some strains of mice that have been inbred ruthlessly for laboratory purposes.

Even worse, the researchers found that the part of the genes responsible for the immune system was similarly lacking in variability. While cheetahs would reject skin grafts from domestic cats in the usual ten or twelve days, they accepted skin grafts from one another as if they were the same animal, sloughing them off only after two or three months. So poor an immune system places the cheetah at risk from viral attacks, which come along in new forms all the time. In 1982, a viral disease called "feline infectious peritonitis" struck the cheetahs at the Wildlife Safari Park in Oregon. While the disease can be rampant in domestic cats, it kills only about 10 percent of the affected group. In Oregon, and later in other parks, eighteen cheetahs — half the population — died.

How had this come about? Cheetah behavior would seem to dictate against inbreeding: they do not remain with their offspring once they are grown. Males are territorial, while females wander through several territories. The answer may be discovered in the fossil record which shows that several species of cheetah lived worldwide until the end of the Ice Age, when various events brought about a massive extinction of mammals. The cheetah population, perhaps more than others, was decimated, and its range restricted to parts of Africa. Possibly, the catastrophe caused a severe population "bottleneck" — a situation where only a handful of cheetahs remained, and generations of inbreeding necessarily resulted. In fact, peering at the fine details of cheetah genetics, researchers speculate that, for reasons unknown, there may have been more than one bottleneck in cheetah history.

There is hope, of course. Other animals have survived such bottlenecks. The northern elephant seal was hunted to near extinction and only twenty remained in 1922, when protective legislation was passed. Today, off the coasts of Mexico and California, there are tens of thousands, one of nature's spectacles. In all, there are probably about 20,000 cheetahs, including a subspecies in the eastern part of Africa that has proven to be slightly less inbred than those to the south. Cross-breeding the two subspecies will almost surely prove beneficial, and since this must, for the most part, be done in captivity, where cheetahs breed poorly, it may be the brave new techniques of artificial reproduction will give these — and many other animal species — a continued lease on life.

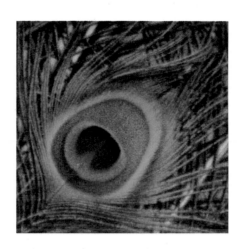

Animals of Australia and the Indian Subcontinent

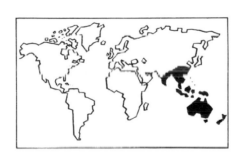

Although endangered in the wild, several species of tiger (*Panthera tigris*) are, if anything, too numerous in captivity. From the point of view of species management, this abundance poses difficult problems: to limit the number now by using contraceptives or other means may lead to an age imbalance in the captive population.

Some species of tiger (*Panthera tigris*) kept in captivity now outnumber their relatives in the wild. A coordinated effort by zoos to respond to the diminishing wild populations has resulted in decisions like that taken recently by the Edinburgh Zoo, to cease breeding Bengal tigers for which it was well known, and take on the more seriously endangered Siberian tiger.

◁ The Malayan sun bear (*Helarctos malayanus*), a native of southeast Asian rain forests and consequently threatened as the forest is destroyed, is the smallest of all bear species. A recently-installed exhibit at San Diego Zoo, Sun Bear Forest, features five of the bears, with lion-tailed macaques and a variety of birds, in a tropical setting.

△ The sloth bear (*Melursus ursinus*) is difficult to exhibit because, as its name implies, it tends to sleep a great deal. Efforts by zoo staff to stimulate the bear into activity that is useful to the animal and enjoyable to the visitor have met with limited success. At Minnesota, honey was smeared in crevices and crannies near the bear's den, but it became so efficient at scooping up the delicacy that it was able to return to dozing within minutes.

▷ The straw-necked ibis (*Threskiornis spinicollis*) is relatively common in zoos and not yet considered to be endangered in the wild. Where the bird is systematically bred, the technique of "double clutching," that is, removing the first and second clutches of eggs for artificial incubation and allowing the parents to raise the third, permits a relatively high rate of production.

▷ Now classed as vulnerable in the IUCN *Red Data Book*, the markhor (*Capra falconeri*) is kept at a relatively small number of zoos where, however, its rate of increase appears to be stable.

◁ The Celebes black ape or black macaque (*Cynopithecus niger*) is a thick-set and gregarious monkey. In its native range, the northeast portion of the Celebese Islands, groups of several dozen congregate around a dominant male and defend their territory vigorously.

A black leopard or black panther (*Panthera pardus*) prowls
through the rain forest gallery in the Bronx Zoo's Jungle
World. The color is a genetic accident: the black leopard
is not a separate species but, simply, a leopard that
happens to be black.

Although more adaptable in the wild than some of the other great cats, the black leopard (*Panthera pardus*) is increasingly suffering from the loss of habitat that affects others of its kind.

◁ The Sumatran orangutan (*Pongo pygmaeus abelii*) is severely endangered — there may be three or four thousand left within its range in the Indonesian archipelago. Ironically, the zoo population is increasing to the point where there will soon be too little space to accommodate more.

△ The orangutan (*Pongo pygmaeus*) is highly intelligent and always popular with zoo-goers. It is also endangered. According to one estimate, at the current rate at which hardwood forest is being destroyed, the orangutan's domain will have vanished by the end of the century.

△▷ The Royal Zoological Society of Antwerp and Jersey Zoo
are among several zoos working to build a stable captive
population of babirusa (*Babyrousa babyrussa*) which is now
endangered in its native Indonesia. Although similar in
appearance to wild pig, it is a distinct species bearing
some zoological resemblance also to the hippopotamus.

The most spectacular member of the pigeon family, the Victoria crowned pigeon (*Goura victoria*) is one of many birds seen in the Australasian Pavilion of the Metropolitan Toronto Zoo.

The emu (*Dromaius novaehollandiae*), this one in its paddock in the Metropolitan Toronto Zoo, is well established in zoos around the world: virtually all on exhibit are descended from captive birds.

The Asiatic elephant (*Elephus maximus*) is almost done for, both because of the destruction of its habitat and poaching for ivory. It is one of the fifty species on the SSP list of the AAZPA.

One of the earliest Species Survival Plans was developed for the Siberian tiger (*Panthera tigris*). As a consequence of this attention, by 1988, 100 Siberian tigers in North American zoos had changed residence at least once. Tigers in European zoos have been similarly mobile.

△ The highly-strung proboscis monkey (*Nasalis larvatus*) is exceedingly delicate, requiring warmth and a humid atmosphere in order to flourish. Only in fairly recent years have zoos in such cold climates as that of the Bronx developed the technical facilities to accommodate them.

△ The red or lesser panda (*Ailurus fulgens*) is on the list of the AAZPA for special attention under the Species Survival Plan. There are about 160 in captivity (outside of China): the National Zoological Park in Washington, the Bronx, Kansas City, Minnesota and Toronto zoos are among those actively participating in the program.

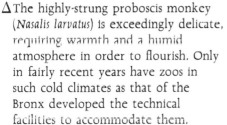

◁ The koala (*Phascolarctos cinerus*) is a woolly, tail-less marsupial — and not related to the bear family. It is an extremely fussy eater. It doesn't just require eucalyptus leaves: different species of koala require different species of eucalyptus. Few zoos outside of Australia are equipped to deal with such fine distinctions: San Diego Zoo is one of half a dozen in North America.

The sarus crane (*Grus antigone*), one of the largest of cranes,
is indigenous to southern Asia and India. The New
York Zoological Society, the National Zoological Park
in Washington and the Jersey Zoo are among zoos
maintaining significant breeding groups of this bird.

Few animals native to Australia are now exported due to
the stringent controls that have been imposed by the
Australian government. A few species of wallaby can be
seen in European and North American zoos, but nothing
to compare with the variety in Taronga, Sydney, or the
Royal Melbourne Zoological Gardens.

The most spectacular of pheasants, the male peafowl (*Pavo cristatus*) is native to India and Sri Lanka, but common as an ornamental bird throughout Europe and North America. It is frequently given the run of zoological gardens.

Breeding the long-tailed glossy starling
(*Lamprotornis mevesii purpureus*) is a
project of the Jersey Wildlife
Preservation Trust.

△ ▷ The Zoological Society of London at Whipsnade (shown) has one of the best records in the world for breeding rhinos, including the great Indian rhinoceros (*Rhinoceros unicornis*). The studbook for the species is maintained at the Basel Zoo in Switzerland.

Endangered in the wild, the Malayan tapir (*Tapirus indicus*) has found a home in a number of zoos — Copenhagen, Oklahoma, St. Louis and San Diego to name a few — where it is successfully bred.

Despite the lethal appearance of its long snout, the gavial or gharial (*Gavialis gangeticus*) is usually harmless to humans. In its native range, in the waters of the Ganges and some other Indian rivers — where it is severely endangered — it feeds on fish.

The Sumatran rhinoceros (*Dicerorhinus sumatrensis*), like the other Asian rhinos, is on the verge of extinction. An international effort is under way to rescue stranded rhinos in the wild and to set up captive breeding programs.

4 · Ten Fine Zoos

Every zoo has its own ambience, a combination of climate, topography, architecture, local culture, taste and money, among other considerations, which also include commitment to the welfare of the animals in the collection. A zoo located in a place of steep hills cannot recreate an African veld; a zoo located in a region with severe winters has to have elaborate buildings if it wishes to display tropical animals; a zoo with a large private support group may be able to accomplish far more by way of basic research than one that depends entirely on municipal funding. Virtually all zoos, including the best zoos, reflect these parameters.

There are some very bad zoos — places where a kind of depression sets in, tasks of the most ordinary sort are left undone, things get run down and animals are harmed and people disgraced. These are relatively few and found less and less often, because zoo associations, humane groups and people in general simply won't put up with such a place for long. It is probably fair to say that the terrible zoo is an endangered species . . . unless one is inclined to think of any animal in captivity as a prisoner and therefore that all zoos are terrible. But the opposite of captive for animals is not *free* but *wild*, and that is a very different state altogether, especially from the standpoint of the welfare of a given individual animal.

Of course, in a perfect world, all wild animals would be left in the wild, with the opportunity to reproduce and carry on their

Jungle World in the Bronx Zoo.

kind, thanks to a plentiful habitat and the bounty of nature — but our world isn't perfect. It has been very different since the arrival of human beings who, with some promptness, domesticated plants, then dogs from wolves, chickens from jungle fowl, pigs from wild boar and so forth. These animals are not technically considered captive, but they certainly aren't wild either — and certainly not free in any usual sense of the word. Few moments in any wild animal's life are free. Some mammals and birds are, especially when young, free to play, though some zoologists believe that to call such activity "play" is to anthropomorphize it: it might more accurately be called "practice" — *necessary* practice. In fact, wild animals live lives of constant and fearful necessity: constant attention to the whereabouts of food, to the potential of attack by predators, the continuing problems of migration, of territorial defense, of living with parasites. What pet dog does not still show an awareness of these matters, even after thousands of years of association with humanity? Most animal reactions to such situations and needs are governed by instinctive responses, though learning is possible in many species — and such can hardly be called freedom. It makes little sense at all to look at zoos with such considerations in mind. What makes sense is to ask if the animals in a zoo are treated with respect, if they are content, and since few animals can answer a direct question of that sort, one has to look to other evidence.

A lone female elephant in a zoo exhibit is almost certainly not healthy mentally, since in nature, female elephants tend to live in close-knit herds and need company. Elephants also tend to be fairly active animals and need what even might be called challenges to be content. And more and more, zoos employ highly trained elephant keepers to put these creatures through one or another set of paces — demonstrations of strength or agility, workouts, obedience tests. This is usually entertaining and educational for zoo visitors, but, more importantly, it is entertaining for the elephants. That the keepers, wielding sticks with hooks on the end, are the authorities, bossing the elephants around, offering praise when it is due and punishment when the rules are broken, is different only in physical scale from someone handling a horse. Elephants have worked for people for millennia. The question is, can we work for them now that they clearly need help? And that is where the modern zoo comes in.

Longevity of zoo animals is almost invariably higher than that of individuals in the wild. It stands to reason. Captive animals are better fed. They are free of predation and most parasites. They have medical care of increasing sophistication. (Zoo vets can now even mend the broken legs of such fragile creatures as dik-diks or birds.) The animals in zoos do not need to compete among themselves for resources. Severely stressed animals rarely breed successfully.

In addition to more natural-looking habitats, zoos are paying greater attention to the animals' diets. In one study of blood samples of captive rhinoceroses at the Bronx Zoo, the zoo population was found to be anemic and to have a much lower level of Vitamin E than those in the wild. Working in cooperation with zoo staffers, biologists in the field collected blood and fecal samples of wild populations, as well as samples of their diet and other clues to their eating habits. For other finicky species, that only eat one kind of leaf or insect for example, or whose range of foods is impossible to supply, zoo keepers strive to duplicate the nutritional content of the natural diet. Many zoo animals are fed pellets that contain the required balance of protein, fiber and carbohydrate, along with fresh fruit, nuts, vegetables and other treats provided as a supplement.

Information about zoo animals diets is now also being computerized and shared among zoos from many countries. This can be especially important for rare captive species and for vulnerable newborns. Keepers have found that such things as the shape of a feeding tray or other behavioral characteristics may decide whether or not an animal eats what's provided. Food is sometimes hidden so that the animal has to search for and find it, more or less as it would in the wild. Others refuse to eat off the floor. By collecting and sharing such information, zoos hope to improve the health, and the ability to breed, of captive animals.

Yes, one might say, they are content, these well-fed, well-cared-for, long-lived zoo animals. Then comes the question, arising from some atavistic sense that there is a scale of nature, some sense that "free" and "wild" mean the same thing, that domestic is somehow bad: aren't zoo animals somehow *tame* or tamed? And isn't that wrong? After generations of living in ease in a zoo, is a tiger or a monkey still a tiger or a monkey, or is it some lesser breed?

There is ample concrete evidence — for example, maulings, and even worse, by zoo animals of people who got too close to an escaped animal or, more typically, stuck a hand (or more) into an enclosure — that even after several generations of life in a zoo many wild instincts are intact. Does captivity mean domestication? *Un*wildness? One need only look at the increasing number of successful introductions of zoo animals to the wild to know that doing time in a zoo does not render an animal necessarily unfit for the wilderness life.

Generally speaking, the people who work in zoos have taken all of these questions into consideration and have reached their own conclusions. These conclusions show up in the fact of their daily actions. While human-crowd management may be the most complex matter any zoo deals with, its chief and overriding concern is the care of the animals. Only when this aspect of zoo management has been worked out does a zoo have the luxury of doing research or evolving conservation measures or performing a public-education function. Like any human institution, a zoo is full of human ambition, sin and politics. There is always a lot of gossip, as in any small town. But there is also something a bit remote and unworldly, a bit apart and above it all, about being on the inside of a zoo, working there. A great deal can happen in the world at large but none of it really counts for much if, say, the bongo's shed needs to be shoveled out, or the yellow-naped parrot is having breathing problems, or the tree kangaroo is making nesting motions and may have joeys tonight. Local politics, national politics, international politics — none of these is, as of the moment, as commanding to the people who work in a zoo as an animal showing signs of trouble. These are, of course, animal people.

A zoo vet, asked to name the most difficult animal to deal with, replied without hesitation, "Human." Yet, zoo people are not philosophers. They are activists. They go into the enclosures every day and sniff the environment and clean up. Even when they graduate to curator and beyond, they tend to like to get out of the office and sniff around a little. Generally speaking, you could show zoo people the delights of foreign places and they would probably nod and head immediately to the zoo, strike up a conversation with a keeper there, and remember their trip abroad with great fondness.

Visitors to zoos do not necessarily lay eyes on a great research zoologist (though one may be working there) or a zoo vet or any other bigshot. They see the animals and, usually in the course of their visit, some keepers. If a visitor cannot tell by looking at the animals and their habitat if they are content, then the next best thing is to look at the keepers. If the keepers are content, it's probably a very good zoo.

There are many such in the world. To single out ten from the more than 600 zoos in the world is perhaps an exercise in folly. But these are among the finest, and most of the zoos profiled here have lent special support in the preparation of this book. (See Appendix A for a list of some sixty others and information about their membership programs.) The thumbnail sketches given here are offered to provide a sense of the marvelous variety of zoodom and perhaps lure people to them — or to the nearest zoo at hand. In making such a visit, you will, among other things, be giving witness to an international effort to maintain some of the loveliest masterworks of creation. Better yet, join a local zoo and have your name added to the rolls of those who are actively supporting that effort.

BARCELONA

Barcelona's current zoo was started in 1892, when the city took over a private collection and the mayor ordered that the animals be installed in the Parc de la Ciudadela on the site left vacant after the 1888 World's Fair. The zoo was inaugurated with a small number of animals, among them three pairs of lions, a zebra, bears, camels, and the popular elephant, Avi (Grandpa). That zoo has grown to about 30 acres (12 ha) and houses a major collection of animals.

A stroller through the zoo sees birds from a wide variety of habitats and regions, divided into two major groups — those housed in the aviary and those that adapt more readily to Barcelona's climate and an earthbound life. Nocturnal birds of prey are kept in a darkened room so that they can be observed in action. In many cases, the birds share living space with mammals or move in semifreedom along the paths and throughout the grounds of the zoo.

The zoo's mammal collection includes almost all orders but emphasizes the carnivores and large herbivorous mammals. The zoo has tried to distribute them in a logical manner but, because the zoo is almost 100 years old and its first inhabitants were mammals, later piecemeal improvements have caused some animal groups to be split up. Well-defined groups include the felines, and the group of "African big game" animals, including elephants, rhinos, giraffes, gnus, zebras and hippos. Bears and deer can be seen from a ramp above the African fauna. Most widely dispersed are the large herbivorous animals, which are housed throughout the entire grounds.

The primates are scattered throughout the zoo, the main exhibit being the anthropoid pavilion, home of a famous albino gorilla named Copito de Nieva (Snowflake). Elsewhere are lemurs, black-throated chimps separated from the public by a moat, including several born in the zoo; and an island of South American monkeys who use their tails in getting around a large jungle gym. Another highlight is the high-temperature terrarium with its jungle-like vegetation — home of reptiles and amphibians, including crocodiles, ranging from small South American caimans to the impressive false gavial of the Ganges.

A behind-the-scenes effort is the Rehabilitation Center for Native Birds, devoted to Spanish birds of prey that have been captured, accidentally found or are ill.

Barcelona Zoological Park.

BERLIN

The Berlin Zoological Gardens was founded in 1841 when the Prussian King Friedrich Wilhelm IV presented his pheasantry and animal collection to the citizens of Berlin. A century later it had become one of the most important zoos in the world but, after two bombing raids in the Second World War and brief service as a battlefield at war's end, it was utterly destroyed. Only 91 of 12,000 animals survived. Rebuilt since then, it has again become one of the world's leaders, playing an important role in breeding endangered species including white rhinos; marsh, pampas and Eld's deer; Persian leopards, maned wolves and a variety of rare birds.

Just inside the main gate is the yellow-tiled elephant house, which features a large hall filled with tropical plants. The spacious outdoor enclosures are separated from the public by narrow dry moats. African and Asian elephants are put through a daily performance for the benefit of the public and for their own amusement. Beyond the elephant house is a large artificial lake filled year-round with waterfowl. In summer, an island is home to herons, egrets and cranes, and on a distant peninsula is a breeding colony of flamingos. On yet another island, ring-tailed lemurs from Madagascar spend the summer.

Nearby, in a modernized rodent house, is an active colony of North American prairie dogs and a host of South American rodents, including the world's largest, the capybara, about the size of a small pig. Beyond it, various monkey species, including baboons, clamber over large, natural-seeming rock outcrops that conceal the monkey house. Chimpanzees, gorillas and orangutans inhabit the house for great apes (the first captive-bred orang was born in the Berlin Zoo in 1928), and the monkey house, with its associated tropical house, maintains the other monkeys and macaques, mandrills and lemurs that make up the zoo's primate collection.

Elsewhere, at the bottom of a staircase leading up to the aquarium, stands a life-size statue of an iguanodon, a representative of the dinosaurs that ruled the earth until some sixty million years ago. The demise of the dinosaurs, in a sense, made the world safe for mammals and birds (both of which arose from reptilian ancestors), but on the second floor of the aquarium, a visitor can stand on a bridge amid rich tropical vegetation and look down on the animals that most harken back to the days of dinosaurs: alligators and crocodiles. The zoo's collection includes the Mississippi alligator, including one near-nine-footer (274 cm), and the smaller Chinese alligator (probably the prototype for the legendary Chinese dragon, and today a severely endangered species). Also on hand are the American and Nile crocodiles (both species have bred well in the zoo, with the help of an incubator) and the dwarf caiman, barely three feet (1 m) in length. Nearby, those other reptilian ancients, the giant tortoises from the Galápagos and the Seychelles, lumber about in slow motion.

Along with such zoo favorites as hippos and cheetahs, the zoo maintains corrals for both wild and domestic cattle, from Sri Lanka's

Berlin Zoological Gardens.

dwarf zebu to the huge black water buffalo that does so much of a man's work in Southern Asia. Australian and African owls, as well as more common European ones, regularly breed in aviaries near an exhibition of many of the world's endangered cranes.

Nearby, Bear Rocks serves as home for the heraldric animal of the city of Berlin, the European brown bear. Increasingly rare in the highly populated countries of Europe, the brown bear breeds well in captivity, and it is not unusual to see the mothers bring their cubs out of the indoor enclosures to explore Bear Rocks in early spring. In another area, one sees the black bears that are relatively common in U.S. parks. There is a special set of enclosures for tropical bears, the rarest of which is the spectacled bear, a South American species that has bred frequently at the zoo. Here, too, is the sloth bear of Sri Lanka and India, which feeds chiefly on ants and termites (it has a long tongue) and, uniquely among bears, carries its young on its back. In addition, there is the small, mean-tempered Malayan sun bear, a poor breeder in captivity. Around the corner from the tropical bears is one of the largest polar-bear enclosures in the world, a great island of granite surrounded by water.

In the camel house, one can also see the desert chariot's New World relatives — the vicuna, llama, alpaca and guanaco — as well as flocks of flightless rheas and emus, the latter an Australian bird. Beyond lies the rhino and tapir house with the most impressive array of these beasts in all of Europe. Most valuable are the armor-plated Indian rhinos, which have bred well in the zoo. Indeed, the zoo has had such success with the two African species, the solitary black rhino and the much larger white rhino, that it maintains the studbooks for them both.

A view of the Berlin Zoo photographed by William Mann, director of the National Zoological Park, Washington, between the two world wars.

FRANKFURT

Founded in 1857 to provide the citizens of Frankfurt with a "living textbook of natural history," the Frankfurt Zoo has long had a policy of showing its visitors a representative cross-section of the animal world rather than a large number of animals. It was here that captive clouded leopards first successfully raised their own young, and once zoo officials found that cheetahs were made skittish by the proximity of other big cats, they put them by themselves amid enclosures with such African species as sable antelope and ostriches, and the cheetahs began to breed. The other big cats — tigers, lions, jaguars, leopards — are housed in the carnivore house, which had to be rebuilt after the war's bombing raids. It was rebuilt on the original 1874 foundations, but was greatly enlarged, with outdoor enclosures. Since subdominant members of a pride of African lions are often oppressed by the dominant members, their enclosure is bisected by natural rock, providing the subdominant animals a means to get out of sight of their "superiors."

The zoo features an exotarium, a large building that includes climatic panoramas, large aquaria, reptile halls, a section for poisonous snakes and a crocodile jungle. Elsewhere, a children's zoo features donkeys, Shetland ponies, pygmy horses and goats, and Vietnamese pot-bellied pigs.

Perhaps the zoo's most unusual exhibit is Grzimek House, named for former zoo director Bernard Grzimek, a well-known champion of wildlife who wrote many internationally popular books on the subject. When it came time to rebuild the small mammal house, the zoo took note of the fact that, of the eighteen orders of mammals, only a third are diurnal; the rest are active at night and thus are rarely, if ever, seen in zoos. Thus, the major portion of Grzimek House is given over to nocturnal animals. A visitor is ushered into a dark world and, after the fifteen minutes it takes for the eyes to adjust totally, you see representatives of ten nocturnal orders of mammals, as well as a number of birds that are active at night, particularly kiwis, owls and nightjars, going about their business. Among the mammals are the egg-laying spiny anteater, an aerial marsupial called the sugar glider, tenrecs, various bats, lemurs and galagos, jerboas, fennec foxes, civets, kinkajous, sloths, the aardvark and aardwolf. Thus, Grzimek House provides an introduction to a large number of mammals that most people may never have heard of, much less seen, and that remain among the least understood.

In the daylight section, mongooses, lynxes, howler monkeys and various tamarins live among a variety of birds. One of the more peculiar mammals is the little rock hyrax, which looks like an agile climbing rodent but is actually a distant relative of the elephant.

Elsewhere in the zoo, African enclosures show, on the one side, the inhabitants of the African savannah, such as the ostrich and the formidable antelope called the sable, and, on the other side, cheetahs and Cape hunting dogs. These dogs, with their broad heads, resemble but are not related to hyenas; they hunt in packs and only at certain periods of the day. Typically, captive individuals, if they breed in zoos, do not rear their young, which have to be given to surrogate domestic dogs to raise, but the Frankfurt Zoo's hunting dogs have been raising their own young since 1977.

Beyond the African enclosures is a large thicket of dense bushes. Visitors who venture in find themselves in a series of cleverly arranged aviaries where such birds as whale-headed storks and boat-billed herons can mingle with people or withdraw, as they wish. Other inhabitants are various species of pheasant, ibis, egret, as well as avocets and oystercatchers.

At the monkey house, in one of four open-air enclosures, hamadryas baboons live on a replica of a granite outcrop of the kind that towers up here and there in the Serengeti Plain. At the other end of the house, rhesus monkeys spend the day on sandstone rocks, next door to spider monkeys confined by an attractive narrow moat. The zoo has had considerable success in breeding endangered monkeys, such as Goeldi's monkey and the cotton-head marmoset. The zoo has also had great success breeding the largest and heaviest of apes, the lowland gorilla, as well as chimps and orangutans. And with the successful breeding of the extremely rare and endangered bonobo, or pygmy chimpanzee, Frankfurt became the first zoo to succeed in the regular breeding of all four kinds of ape. Their offspring have gone to zoos all over the world. Frankfurt was the first zoo to use massively heavy glass (1970) to surround a gorilla enclosure, allowing the animals to venture outdoors and giving visitors a good view. One can also peer through the window of the animal nursery and watch baby apes and other animals that, for one reason or another, have to be hand-reared by human foster parents.

Elsewhere, a band of North American prairie dogs, which are rodents, has designed their own place, digging subterranean burrows where they please within their enclosure. Extremely active and affectionate with each other, they are favorites with children, as is an elaborate maze cut out of privet bushes.

Sable antelope, Frankfurt Zoo.

JERSEY

Established in 1963 by internationally known writer and zoologist Gerald Durrell, the Jersey Wildlife Preservation Trust is perhaps the only zoo that devotes the vast majority of its time and energy to aiding and breeding threatened animal species. Located on the grounds of a manor on the Channel island of Jersey, it is a unique sanctuary (though visitable) where colonies of endangered species have been built up into reservoirs against extinction.

A chief focus of interest is the island of Mauritius in the Indian Ocean, east of Madagascar, home of the now extinct dodo, which the Trust chose as its emblem. The Trust is engaged in returning captive-bred specimens of the pink pigeon to Mauritius and has been breeding rare species of skink, gecko and boa found only on a small island near Mauritius and almost doomed by the introduction of goats and rabbits and the subsequent destruction of vegetation. With the alien animals eradicated, the Trust awaits the natural revegetation of the island to release the reptiles back in the wild.

Spectacularly successful with endangered pheasants and other birds, the Trust bred the white-eared pheasant up from a captive population (outside of China) of about 20 to today's population of 500 in the world's zoos. The Trust is also part of the international effort to return the Bali mynah to its native habitat, and thick-billed parrots bred at Jersey have been returned to their native pine woods in Arizona. Spectacled bears, a South American species, and the odd, pig-like Indonesian babirusa have bred successfully on the manor grounds, and the Trust maintains breeding groups of several species of lemurs, as well as a research station on Madagascar for fieldwork and the training of local biologists on behalf of these endangered primates.

The list of animals at the Jersey Trust, indeed, resembles a Who's Who of endangered species, including many that are on Species Survival Plans — even the humble snail. On the island of Moorea, in the South Pacific's Society Islands, there once were literally millions of snails per square mile — in all, many species of Partula — various species in different valleys, a study in what evolutionary biologists call "adaptive radiation." But an American carnivorous snail was introduced to the island and spread rapidly, devouring the resident snails, heading them toward extinction.

The Trust's Gaherty Reptile Breeding Centre consists of spacious units, each arranged to suit the particular animal (the Costa Rican plumed basilisk, for example, dwells in a unit that resembles its rain forest habitat), which is not only good for breeding but makes for excellent exhibition. Here one can see the twist-neck terrapin, oriental water dragon, rhinoceros iguana and reticulated python.

Marmosets and tamarins have bred happily at Jersey, along with the closely related (and threatened) Goeldi's monkey. From an original importation of six of the latter, the Trust had recorded sixty births over a period of ten years, supplying such zoos as Frankfurt, Los Angeles, London, Chicago (Brookfield) and Washington, D.C.,

where the monkeys have gone on to produce yet other generations.

There are more bats in the world than any other kind of mammal and one doesn't think of them as being endangered, but the Rodrigues fruit bat — found only on a southwest Indian Ocean island of the same name — fell to only 150 individuals in the 1970s, the result of habitat loss. Gerald Durrell collected 18 and in a decade had brought his captive population to more than 50. The main group can be seen in a specially designed nocturnal house, where the day-and-night cycle has been reversed for the benefit of visitors. Others have access to a large outdoor aviary, fresh air and natural light. The Trust is making comparative studies to determine the long term-effects of artificial conditions such as the nocturnal display on these animals.

The Jersey Wildlife Preservation Trust's dodo logo.

Visitors to Jersey can wander through much of the grounds and observe many animals in an elegant setting. Perhaps no animal draws as much attention as Jambo, a male lowland gorilla born in the Basel Zoo in 1961, the first male gorilla born in captivity and raised by its mother. At Jersey, by 1988, Jambo had sired sixteen offspring and was a grandfather, making him probably the most prolific gorilla in captivity. On one occasion he demonstrated remarkable compassion by protecting a young visitor who had fallen into the enclosure — a vast playground where family groups or individuals occupy themselves playing or foraging for food hidden in the grass. The Trust's success with these apes has been such that it manages the regional studbook of the species.

In addition to its breeding activities, the Trust has run an international training center since 1978 at which students from some thirty-five countries have studied the techniques of captive-animal breeding and wildlife management.

The Monkey House, London Zoo, about 1835 by George Scharf.

LONDON

Founded by Sir Stamford Raffles in 1826 for the benefit of science, the Zoological Society of London opened the Zoological Gardens in Regent's Park the following year, the first truly modern zoo. It has pioneered in many ways ever since, including opening the first reptile house and the first aquarium. Indeed, it was a London music-hall artist, the Great Vance, who evidently coined the word "zoo" in a song that went: "Walking in the Zoo is an okay thing to do."

The London Zoo has a long history of research, formerly into taxonomy (the classification of species) but currently in the areas of genetics, disease, nutrition, reproduction and veterinary science. Its zoological library is considered among the most complete in the world. In 1931, it opened the first open-air zoo, a 500-acre (200 ha) park at Whipsnade, 30 miles (48 km) north of the city, in the countryside, where animals can roam relatively freely. With this installation and a strong commitment to conservation, the London Zoological Society has become a leader in breeding captive animals.

It was from Whipsnade that Père David's deer were returned to China, many of them hand-reared in the Whipsnade children's zoo. The first second-generation captive-born cheetahs in the world were born at Whipsnade, which was also one of the first breeding centers outside of Africa to attain a sizable herd of white rhinos. The first captive Chilean flamingos hatched there in 1975. In all, 80 percent of the 2,000 animals at Whipsnade were born and reared there.

Visitors can walk through much of the park, drive around the perimeter or take the Whipsnade and Umfolozi Railway, an old train that goes through a large area given over mainly to Asian ungulates (this is the best way to see the white rhinos as well). Throughout the park, many of the animals — including Chinese water deer, prairie marmots, peafowl, guinea fowl, North American turkeys, Indian jungle fowl and wallabies — wander freely, mingling with the visitors. A family center is home for a children's zoo; a water-mammals exhibit, where bottle-nosed dolphins can be seen swimming under water and performing; and a bird-of-prey show; outlying areas maintain animals of Africa and of the North.

The London Zoo itself is, among other things, home of Chia-Chia, a male giant panda that has sired offspring in the Madrid Zoo by means of artificial insemination. The zoo has recently undergone extensive change and it is now a far cry from the place where the famous Jumbo lived, the huge African elephant (over 11 feet [335 cm] tall) that was eventually bought by P.T. Barnum and whose name became synonomous with gigantic things. The area called Mappin Terraces, which used to house a variety of wild boars and bears (in one of the earliest uses of open, moated enclosures), has been converted to an arctic wilderness where polar bears can meander and swim among rocky slopes, deep pools and icebergs. There is an underwater observation area where visitors can observe the bears when they swim. Other highlights of the arctic exhibit are birds of prey, swans, geese, ducks, otters, and arctic foxes. Under the Mappin Terraces of old, the zoo had built an aquarium, which was refurbished as an invertebrate exhibit, while a new aquarium includes a spectacular Pacific coral reef, replete with its brightly colored denizens.

The New Lion Terraces, where the big cats live in areas that are rich with plant life similar to that in their natural habitats, opened in 1976. The tigers are to be seen among tall, reedy plants that grow near water in the tropics, while the lions are in an open, grassy enclosure reminiscent of the plains of Africa. A large new building with connected paddocks houses giraffes and camels. Tasmanian devils, echidnas, springhaas (a hopping rodent), kinkajous and fennec foxes patrol an artificial night in the zoo's Moonlight World, along with bush babies and bats.

A children's zoo features mostly domestic animals — goats and sheep, which were probably the first animals to be domesticated (the sheep are sheared each summer, and children can mingle with the goats during the year); Friesian cows that are milked daily;

The Snowdon free-flight aviary,
overlooking the canal, in Regent's
Park, London.

pigs, rabbits, guinea pigs and geese. Nearby are reproductions of Pleistocene cave paintings, showing the ancestors of some of the animals that were to become today's domesticated creatures. Children can also take rides in carts drawn by ponies, camels and llamas and handle bones, skulls and other objects that circulate through the zoo on trolleys. During the summer, various animals are brought into the open Hummingbird Amphitheatre to be introduced and discussed.

Though not especially recent, a continuingly popular feature of the zoo is the Snowdon Aviary, a vast flight cage of many facets and angles with numerous habitats, designed by the former husband of Princess Margaret. A cantilevered bridge that spans the aviary takes the visitor above grass, cliff face, running water, trees and bushes — different ecosystems that allow from 150 to 200 birds to live together throughout the year.

NEW YORK

Born in 1899, the Bronx Zoo was the first child of the New York Zoological Society, now responsible also for the Central Park Zoo, the New York Aquarium, a wildlife survival center on a barrier island off Georgia, and a research and conservation action group called Wildlife Conservation International, which in turn sponsors projects in dozens of countries around the world. With 265 acres (107 ha) of woods, ponds, streams and parklands, the Bronx Zoo is by far the largest urban zoo in the country and it has taken advantage of its real estate to provide a variety of simulated habitats on a grand scale.

An overhead train, Skyfari, takes visitors above African plains where predator and prey, safely separated by moats, are exhibited together: lions, gazelle, antelope, cheetah, giraffe, zebra, ostrich. A monorail, the Bengali Express, runs through a 40-acre (16 ha) simulation of the dark forests and open meadows of Asia, populated with elephants, rhinos, sitka deer, antelope, Siberian tigers — in all, more than 1,000 animals of more than 100 species, all roaming about in seeming freedom. Associated with this Wild Asia exhibit is the Wild Asia Plaza, modeled on an Asian bazaar, where visitors can ride camels among pagoda-roofed pavilions and learn about endangered species in an open-air theater.

At 2:00 PM each day, the rain begins to fall in Jungle World, an indoor Asian rain forest re-created on a grand scale, that also includes a mangrove swamp and a bit of scrub forest, where giant "dragon lizards" (monitors) sun themselves and burrow in lava outcrops. In the Mangrove Gallery, mudskippers (fish) live on land among hand-sculpted mangrove trees that "grow" in saltwater, and proboscis monkeys cavort on a rocky outcrop. In the rain-forest gallery — 300 feet (91 m) long and 55 feet (16 m) high — thirty species of tropical trees, and scores of shrubs, vines, orchids and ferns are supplemented by artificial plants and outcrops and one of the world's biggest naturalistic murals to create a forest of remarkable verisi-

Baldy, the chimpanzee, is shown here with his keeper at the Bronx Zoo, June 1908.

militude. Here silvered-leaf monkeys, white-cheeked gibbons, black leopards, Malayan tapirs, turtles and many kinds of birds live among natural mosses, vines and flowering plants. In a special gallery called "The Unseen Multitude," one can see the specially adapted amphibians, reptiles, crabs and insects that account for the greater part of rain-forest diversity. Finally, a river tumbles down rocks in a Lower Montane Rain Forest, interrupted by a series of pools filled with narrow-snouted gharials, an Indian crocodile. Throughout the exhibit, visitors' attention is drawn to plaques indicating the rate at which such forests are disappearing.

As an example of concentrated diversity within one group of animals, the Mousehouse, remodeled from the old Small Mammal House, shelters twenty-eight species of rodents — mice, rats, gerbils, squirrels, mongoose, two predators (a skunk and a snake) and a rodent look-alike (a rabbit) are displayed behind glass in naturalistic settings. In a children's zoo, along with the traditional domestic animals one gets to see and touch, one can explore a giant spider web, a hollow log and a prairie-dog tunnel to learn about animal homes. Young visitors can don the ears of a fennec fox (greatly enlarged and electronically operated) to gain insight into animal senses; smell a skunk and escape down a hollow tree to learn of animal defenses; and compete in jumping contests with a bullfrog and crawl into a giant snail shell to explore animal locomotion.

Other highlights at the Bronx Zoo include the World of Darkness, the first exhibit to reverse night and day, and the World of Birds, which innovated in naturalistic habitats, including treetop exhibits, and a three-story aviary where birds fly free.

A major new habitat exhibit is the Himalayan Highlands, which re-creates the high passes and remote mountaintops of Asia in six separate exhibit areas. More than 2,000 plants, trees, shrubs and grasses of 74 species cover more than 2 acres (0.8 ha), in which the natural landscape is supplemented by trees and rocks made of steel, concrete and epoxy. Here one wanders along rocky trails and sees tragopan pheasants, white-naped cranes (the Oriental symbol of fidelity), red pandas and the elusive snow leopard. The zoo has a special interest in the snow leopard, being in charge of its Species Survival Plan and having bred fifty-five cubs in the last two decades, supplying the animal to zoos in six other countries.

A leader in captive breeding in general, the zoo's center on St. Catherines Island in Georgia has bred forty endangered species, including antelopes, marsupials, primates, tortoises and a host of birds. One of these, a large fowl-like bird from Sulawesi in Indonesia is called the maleo. An endangered species, the maleo hen lays its single egg beside a geothermal vent to be warmed by either the sun or the steam. Recently scientists at the center were able to duplicate these effects and produced the first maleo chick outside of Sulawesi. The center is in the forefront of efforts to preserve the red-fronted macaw and a long list of other vulnerable or endangered birds and mammals.

SAN DIEGO

Founded in 1916 in the salubrious climate of Southern California, the San Diego Zoo has become one of the most popular in the world. Thanks to the climate, there never was any need for the kind of vast, heated buildings that were common in most European and North American zoos and are only recently being done away with. Instead, the San Diego Zoo has a wide-open feel, built on rolling hills and canyons in Balboa Park, near the Pacific. From the beginning, the zoo pioneered in open enclosures and moats. Fifty years ago, the zoo's 100 acres (40 ha) were scrub-covered: today, towering eucalyptus, graceful palms, bird-of-paradise and hibiscus cover the grounds, along with orchids and other flowers. The zoo is, in effect, a botanical garden as well.

A major renovation program is aimed at creating a variety of simulated habitats to immerse visitors in a particular ecological system. Such is the zoo's new African Rock Kopje (pronounced copy) exhibit, an outcrop of volcanic lava found jutting up from the African plains. These rock islands teem with life-forms such as the klipspringer, a small antelope at home on the rocks, and the pancake tortoise, a soft-shelled species that withdraws not into its shell but into cracks in the rocks for protection.

Along the newly opened western edge of the zoo, a visitor passes by another bioclimatic experience — bird and plant exhibits. A sparse, dry African savannah is populated by huge milky eagle owls. Striated caracaras reign over a typical Falkland Island grassland. Spectacled owls preside over a subtropical scene. Five tropical cages host a rainbow of birds — bright orange cocks of the rock, yellow and black troupials, toucans and others.

Among the newest of these habitat exhibits is Tiger River, a 3-acre (1 ha) simulation of an Asian tropical rain forest that includes 5,000 plants and 100 animals, along with five waterfalls and a fogging device with 300 outlets that creates a mist so fine that it takes only 5 gallons (23 l) of water a day to create the sensation of rain-forest humidity. As one walks down a dry riverbed under a canopy of palm and fig trees, one is abruptly in the midst in a canyon with waterfalls, pools, marshes and a mud wallow. Fragrant jasmine vines and gingers help visitors smell the rain forest; there is an island of diverse ferns; mature trees — ficus, palms, coral — have been moved from other zoo areas and from as far away as Hawaii. Crocodiles, pythons and Chinese water dragons ply the watery areas, while Sumatran tigers, tapirs, web-footed fishing cats and tarsiers are among the mammalian inhabitants. Ibises, laughing thrushes, whistling ducks, pigeons, leafbirds, lapwings, kingfishers and mynahs are among the brilliant array of birds that flutter through the humid air or patrol the ground.

Yet another tropical forest will be erected in the bottom half of Bear Canyon, testimony to the importance this zoo, like so many others, places on educating people about the rapid loss of this most diverse and valuable ecosystem. It will take another decade at least

before the entire zoo is converted to ecosystem exhibits.

San Diego is one of the most user-friendly of zoos: bus tours cover most of its 100 acres (40 ha) and an aerial tram, called Skyfari, takes one from the eastern edge of the zoo to the western edge, as high as 170 feet (52 m) above the sea-lion pool, Horn and Hoof Mesa, the great-ape grottos, a huge flight cage and Monkey Mesa. There are daily shows of Channel Islands seals, predators of various kinds, and a children's zoo where one can see surrogate human mothers raising baby animals, look at macaws through kaleidoscopes, and pat hoofed stock.

Thirty miles (48 km) north of the city is the zoological society's San Diego Wildlife Park, an 1,800-acre (730 ha) open zoo. Here animals roam almost entirely free in four different habitats — an African and an Asian plain and Asian and South African waterholes. A monorail whisks visitors around the periphery of these areas. Gorillas are to be seen in a splendid exhibition on some loose grassy turf. Special tours in flatbed trucks, called Photo Safaris, take tourists right up to many animals such as rhinos, giraffes and ostriches. This park, while an immensely popular attraction, has also permitted the zoo to undertake large-scale husbandry of endangered species, in particular, ungulates. Probably the largest herd of white rhinos outside of Africa lives here. Together, the park and zoo retain the largest staff of veterinarians of any zoo in the country, and they have had a long commitment to research with an emphasis on biomedical matters.

SYDNEY

Taronga is an Australian aboriginal term for "water view," and with its terraced gardens and animal exhibits overlooking a panoramic view of Sydney Harbor, Taronga is often described as the most beautifully situated zoo in the world. Built to replace an older and much smaller zoo, Taronga opened in 1916 after the large mammal collection had been shipped across the harbor by ferry. Even though the First World War was being waged, 66 percent of the entire Sydney population, some 420,000 people, visited the new zoo in its first year. The best way to visit is to follow the route of the original inhabitants and take a ferry across the harbor, to a landing site. From there, a bus takes you up to the top and you can walk down through the zoo to the wharf again. Landscaping is such that, from the harbor, few manmade structures are visible in the zoo, and from inside, Sydney's residential district disappears.

Taronga, like most Australian zoos, specializes in the fauna of Australasia, and for a number of reasons. One is that the fauna of the region is unlike anything else in the world: Australia has long been an isolated place. The native Australian mammal population, for example, is made up of rats and mice, bats, marine mammals, and marsupials and monotremes. Two kinds of monotremes — the duck-billed platypus and several echidna species — are the only mammals that lay eggs like reptiles (but they produce milk, the

San Diego Zoo.

defining characteristic of mammaldom). Both monotreme types are on display at Taronga, the platypus being difficult to maintain as an exhibit animal since it is crepuscular and shy: no platypus eggs have proven fertile at Taronga.

But, it was the marsupials, mammals with pouches for their young, that "took over" the evolutionary field in Australia and the nearby islands such as Tasmania. These radiated into an astonishing number of species and roles — filling most of the niches that placental mammals took elsewhere in the world. Thus, there were carnivorous, predatory marsupials, such as the Tasmanian wolf, and herbivorous marsupials, such as the kangaroo and wallaby. One marsupial, Leadbeater's possum, had been declared extinct until a small group was rediscovered in Victoria in 1961. Taronga was one of several Australian zoos to establish breeding programs for these lively and beautiful little animals in order to save them from extinction. They have bred well in captivity, but their future in the wild is uncertain because of human encroachment on their very limited range.

Among the most popular and endearing animals in the world is the koala (which is not a bear). It feeds almost exclusively on the leaves of tall eucalyptus trees and, in a naturalistic setting in captivity, might be hard to see. At Taronga, the koalas live in an enclosure filled with dead trees that are dressed each day with fresh eucalyptus leaves, while a helical ramp allows visitors to observe them. That it works is attested to by the fact that a sizable number of koalas have been born and reared in the exhibit. Outside of Australian zoos, the koala can only be seen in a few zoos in North America and Japan.

Australia is famous for its kangaroos and wallabies, and Taronga keeps ten of the fifty species, including such rarities as the brush-tailed bettong and the Parma wallaby, with which the zoo has been so successful that it has been releasing surplus animals back into wild reserves.

Another reason Taronga concentrates on Australasian species is that the country has draconian rules about the import of exotic animals — particularly birds and hoofed stock, which can carry disease vectors that would devastate regional fauna and domestic animals. The Australians are also wary of exotics escaping and becoming pests, as happened when rabbits were introduced. Carnivores and primates are allowed, subject to long quarantine periods, and Taronga has one of the largest chimpanzee colonies in the world, along with other apes and monkeys.

Other attractions at Taronga are the aquarium featuring fish from the Great Barrier Reef, and a rain-forest aviary where thirty typical bird species carry on their colorful lives overhead and on the ground. One of these ground birds is the superb lyrebird, an excellent mimic and one of the great singers among nonsongbirds, especially noted for an elaborate mating display. Another bizarre inhabitant is a satin bowerbird. The males of this species build elaborate dwellings lined with colorful objects to attract female mates. The satin bowerbird at Taronga has obliged with a bower decorated with the likes of colored bus tickets and bits of glass — only some 3 feet (90 cm) from the public walkway through the aviary.

Like some far-sighted zoos in North America and Europe, Taronga has established a drive-through sister zoo, the Western Plains Zoo, 300 miles (480 km) northwest of Sydney, in Dubbo. Here, exhibits are arranged according to the continent of origin and, here again, the specialty is Australian animals: large kangaroos and wallabies, long-legged flightless emus and the like. Lakes attract wild water birds, and the entire installation brings in nearly 200,000 human visitors a year, while Taronga's attendance averages about one million.

The Elephant Temple and, beyond it, a view of Sydney, at Taronga Zoo.

TORONTO

Opened in 1974 after nearly a decade of planning and building by the Metropolitan Toronto Zoological Society, the Metro Toronto Zoo replaced an earlier one with nearly 600 acres (243 ha) of tableland and forest. Sprinkled here and there are open paddocked and glass-roofed pavilions in which the animals are displayed in natural environments. The Toronto Zoo is one of the very few in the world that have dispensed altogether with taxonomic arrangements of animals (all the birds here, primates there) to create a zoogeographic zoo so that mammals, birds, fish, reptiles, amphibians, invertebrates and plants are grouped according to where they live in the wild: Africa, Indo-Malaya, North and South America, Eurasia, the Polar region and Australia.

In the Australian Pavilion, one moves from a tropical rain-forest environment, complete with free-flying birds, to a small marsh, and then to a Great Barrier Reef exhibit with colorful reef fish and invertebrates. Nearby are various Australian pythons and kangaroos. The sights and sounds of the Australian night can be experienced in "The Edge of Night" where a variety of marsupials such as the squirrel-like sugar glider, the spiny anteater, the Tasmanian devil, and various birds and amphibians go about their nocturnal affairs.

In the new Mayan Ruins exhibit, which contains a large waterfall, there are macaws, tapir, llamas and jaguar. Spider monkeys affably share their space with capybara, the largest of all rodents. In the Americas Pavilion there are seventy-two species exhibited underground, including beavers and their lodge and river otters in their private pool. Here you can step into a South American jungle with a host of marmosets and tropical birds and reptiles. The Americas Pavilion also includes an Everglades region and American desert exhibits, as well as an aquarium of American aquatic animals.

The Canadian Animal Domain is home to some of North America's largest creatures — grizzlies, wood bison, cougar, lynx, American elk. There is a pack of Arctic wolves and, extremely rare in any zoo because they are hard to maintain, moose. Several moose have been born at the zoo. There is a special pavilion for African elephants, built to house a bull, expectant mothers and mothers with calves. The Toronto Zoo has the largest elephant herd in Canada and, weather permitting, they can be seen year round in their outdoor paddock, complete with a waterhole. A unique playground allows children to compare their athletic skills with those of a variety of animals, and a new Special Events Pavilion has housed a variety of temporary exhibits, such as the largest display of animated dinosaurs in the world, in which sounds and special effects re-created a moving, growling Mesozoic Era.

Throughout the zoo, public walkways at many levels allow the animals to be seen from many viewpoints. When the polar bears are fed at noon, for example, one can watch them from above or watch them swim from underwater viewing windows. Four clearly marked trails take visitors throughout the zoo (around the world):

A Metropolitan Toronto Zoo vehicle in camouflage.

to outdoor paddocks of Asian and African animals; to winter-hardy Eurasian animals; and to the Canadian Animal Domain. Designed of necessity for all seasons, the zoo's broad paths and rolling topography provide a challenging environment for those cross-country skiers who wish to glide among the animals. A monorail and a zoomobile provide more standard transportation.

The zoo is also a botanical garden: 20,000 trees and shrubs have been planted to provide proper geographical backdrops for the paddocks, and the tropical-plant collection — in indoor pavilions — includes nearly 1,000 shrubs and trees and endless groundcover plants along with a large collection of orchids. The African Pavilion contains the only baobab tree growing in Canada; meanwhile, cleverly trimmed apple trees simulate acacias in the African paddocks.

The zoo is deeply engaged in species-survival programs and captive breeding. It houses about fifty different endangered species of mammals, birds, reptiles and fish. Zoo scientists have bred the Puerto Rican crested toad, a creature so rare it was considered extinct until 1980, and have had great success in breeding lowland gorillas, Sumatran orangutans and African elephants. The zoo has succeeded in returning the wood bison to the wilds in Manitoba and was the first zoo in the Western Hemisphere to breed the grey-cheeked hornbill. (The male of this species walls the female into a cavity in a tree where she lays her eggs and raises the young, the male feeding the family through a small hole and releasing them when the young are ready to fly.)

WASHINGTON, D.C.

A part of the Smithsonian Institution, that museum and research complex that has been characterized as the octopus on the Mall, the National Zoo was established in 1899, the first zoo to be founded precisely for the purpose of preserving endangered species — in this instance, the American bison. Today it is probably the most research-oriented zoo in the world. It has performed long-term studies of the behavior and ecology of the tigers and rhinos that

The entrance to the National Zoological Park, Washington.

share a Nepalese reserve, and their effect on the forest and the local human ecology. Studies of the behavior of elephants and primates have helped shape World Bank policy for economic development in Sri Lanka. Linking studies in the field and in captivity have brightened the future of such animals as the maned wolf and tamarins of South America and a host of creatures in Indonesia.

In league with scientists at the Smithsonian's Tropical Research Center in Panama, zoo researchers have played a central role in understanding the ecological and behavioral keys to Central and South American bird migration and the long-evolved relationship of birds to plants. In addition to its pioneering work on inbreeding, the zoo is probably the leading center for research into artificial breeding techniques and the assorted biomedical sciences and their application to wild as well as captive populations, and has been a pioneer in exotic veterinary practice. Such work goes on behind the scenes, however, and for most visitors, the National Zoo is where the pandas live.

Ling-Ling and Hsing-Hsing remain the zoo's most popular exhibit, though an earlier denizen, the original Smokey Bear, a brown bear rescued from a New Mexico forest fire and long the symbol of the U.S. Forest Service, received so much mail when he arrived that he was assigned his own secretary. Another famous resident was Ham, the chimpanzee that learned sign language and served as NASA's first astronaut at the dawn of the Space Age.

Located among the steep slopes and deep valleys of Rock Creek Park, the National Zoo presents various faces to the public, in a sense a walking tour of past and present zoo architecture. Some buildings, such as the Reptile House, were designed and built during the Depression with WPA funds and artists at work: thus, one finds representations of animals in tile work, in floors, in gargoyle-like sculptures. While the interiors of such buildings have been brought up to date, with naturalistic settings for the animals, the exteriors have been preserved, befitting an arm of the history minded Smithsonian.

In the Ape House, gorillas and orangs search jungle-like arenas for food hidden in the substrate while signs identify them — new ones come and go as part of breeding programs — and their relationship to mankind. Down a hill, along a wide esplanade lined with trees, lies Lion Hill, where both lions and tigers loll, the latter from time to time chasing a beer keg into a watery moat. Virtually all of the interior business of caring for the big cats is located underground, inside the hill.

Taking advantage of its Smithsonian connection, the zoo displays such objects as skeletal remains and pterodactyl models alongside the animals, drawing on the collections of the Museum of Natural history and the Air and Space Museum, as well as many of the fine-art museums. In the newly refurbished giraffe quarters (part of the Elephant House), one can see the delicate skeleton of an okapi — giraffe relative — stretching upwards toward the high branches, a demonstration of the evolutionary path an okapi might have followed in order to become as giraffe.

A reproduction of a Ming dynasty painting of a gibbon greets a visitor to the huge "flight" cages where gibbons and siamangs chase each other in astounding aerial acrobatic feats and displays among poles and ropes. A sign consisting of an Egyptian hieroglyph of a bee helps lead one around to the rear of the Reptile House, past a garden planted explicitly for butterflies, to a new exhibit of invertebrates, a reminder that only a tiny fraction of the animals on earth have ever had backbones. Inside, one sees a variety of aquatic invertebrates, such as anemones and octopi in aquaria, a colony of leaf-cutting ants in situ (the nest is cut away so that one can peer into it and watch their activity), giant cockroaches, huge spiders, and a host of other animals including — by using the microscopes and TV monitors provided — the all-important tiny organisms of the soil.

Though somewhat constricted by its setting in Rock Creek Park, the zoo has recently set out to create a number of naturalistic habitats, such as a simulated wetlands where native and exotic waterfowl (and a few wild ones from the surrounding park) ply the dark waters of several ponds, as herons solemnly patrol the reedy shores. An area will soon be given over to an Amazonian tributary and rain forest, emphasizing the importance of the riparian habitat in such places and, by means of underground viewing rooms, showing the jungle's microhabitats as well. Together with this exhibit, a virtual earth-watch center is planned, where the earth's vital statistics will be updated daily. Throughout what officials hope will become not so much a zoo but a "biopark," the message will be the interrelatedness of soil, plant, invertebrate and other animal forms, and the need to preserve the habitats of the world. The zoo will be able to tell the encouraging stories of conservation, as well. For example, having discovered their tendency to stay close to home, the zoo lets a band of golden lion tamarins roam freely in a stand of trees during the summer months. Successfully introduced back into the wild in Brazil, and a symbol of possibilities in conservation, the tamarins that are left free-ranging in the zoo are often reported as escapees by concerned visitors.

To the west, in the rolling foothills of the Blue Ridge Mountains, just south of the town of Front Royal, Virginia, the zoo maintains a 3,000-acre (1215 ha) conservation and research center. There zoo scientists monitor major breeding populations of Père David's deer, scimitar-horned oryxes, red pandas, maned wolves, several crane species and many other endangered species. Each year students of wildlife management from countries in Asia, Africa and South America come to the center for intensive advanced training in field studies, hands-on management and zoo practices, though this area is closed to the public.

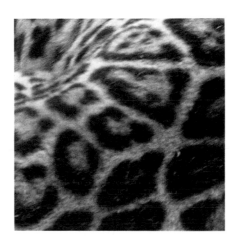

Animals of Central and South America (Neotropical)

△ There have been a number of projects, some funded by World Conservation International, to study the surviving wild jaguars (*Panthera onca*) in Central and South America. As a result of such initiatives jaguar reserves have been established in Belize and elsewhere.

◁ This green iguana (*Iguana iguana*) is a resident of the San Diego Zoo.

▷ Jersey Zoo spearheaded a drive to rescue the severely endangered Goeldi's monkey (*Callimico goeldii*). From an initial importation of six animals, more than sixty births have occurred, making it possible for Jersey to export offspring to form breeding groups elsewhere.

▷ The roseate spoonbill (*Ajaia ajaja*) is not presently regarded as endangered, but its subtle coloring makes it an attractive zoo specimen. Accordingly, it can be seen in the Hanover Zoo, and in a number of American zoos including those in Dallas and New Orleans.

◁ More than eighty zoos are involved in propagating the Andean condor (*Vultur gryphus*). The programs at San Diego, where the more seriously endangered California condor is also being raised, and at the Los Angeles Zoo, have led to the release of captive-reared birds in a national park near Bogota, Colombia.

◁ The zoos in London, Houston, New Orleans and Busch Gardens, Florida, are all raising the startling hyacinthine macaw (*Anodorhynchus hyacinthinus*) with some success.

△ Though not yet endangered, the indications are that the steady destruction of the tropical forest habitat of the harpy eagle (*Harpia harpyja*) will put it at risk before long. A breeding program at the zoo in East Berlin has been reasonably successful.

▷ The king vulture (*Sarcorhampus papa*) of Central and South America is the most brilliantly colored vulture in the world. The Bronx, Los Angeles and San Diego zoos have been among the leaders in breeding this species. The individual shown belongs to the Berlin Zoo.

◁ The Ueno Zoo in Tokyo has had particular success with its breeding colony of scarlet ibis (*Eudocimus ruber*). The Bronx Zoo possesses the specimen shown.

△ As a designated species under the ᴀᴀᴢᴘᴀ Species Survival Plan, a number of zoos are taking an interest in the maned wolf (*Chrysocyon brachyurus*). Frankfurt, the home of this pair, was the first zoo to breed captive animals successfully. The National Zoo at its research center in Virginia has been studying the social organization of a separate group using closed circuit television.

◁ Like the golden lion tamarin, the cotton-headed tamarin (*Saguinus oedipus*) is fast losing its habitat in the forests of Colombia. A number of zoos now keep breeding colonies of the animal. This one was photographed in the marmoset complex of the Jersey Zoo.

5 · The Challenge

When the Spanish conquistador Coronado reached what is now northern Arizona in the 1500s, he came across a large canyon, at the bottom of which was a stream. Routinely, he sent some men down for water, and they were gone a very long time. He had arrived at the Grand Canyon, and there was nothing in his own experience or in the geological perspective to let him know that the stream was a large river and that it was flowing about a mile below him.

Similarly, there is no way for a child watching what he or she knows is called an elephant on a television set to really see how really huge it is. No amount of film footage can substitute for the awe and delight of seeing and smelling one in the flesh, and for that experience most people have to go to a zoo.

Zoos, along with aquariums and game parks, are one of the greatest potential tools available to society to alter the attitudes of a significant proportion of mankind, to create a deep-seated awareness that we are not rightfully the overlords of this planet but share it with a vast and beautiful array of life-forms, each with intrinsic merit. With a proper attention to a conservation message and ethic in its exhibits, zoos of the world have the opportunity to help create almost a quarter of a billion new conservationists each year, and they are beginning to take on the task.

As long as the gates of zoos are open to the public, however, their most important function will continue to be entertainment,

The African bush elephant (*Loxodonta africana*), itself grievously threatened, possesses extraordinary destructive power. A herd of elephants cuts a massive swath through the vegetation it feeds on. The limits to what a given tract of land can support must be closely defined. Even those who seek to preserve wild herds find it necessary to cull them.

and not just for children. Studies in several U.S. zoos and in Frankfurt have confirmed that, contrary to conventional wisdom, by far more adults and teenagers attend zoos than do small children. Yet, a whole generation of people in Europe and North America has grown up amid a plethora of attractive nature books and wildlife films on television. For this sophisticated audience, it is more necessary than ever to have active animals doing interesting things in a naturalistic setting that reflects the animals' natural habitat. One technique, as at the Toronto Zoo and the San Diego Wildlife Park, is the geographic zoo. At Toronto, lions spend time in a large, well-planted enclosure and can see herds of African gazelle next door. Occasionally a lioness will be seen stalking toward the gazelles. The Dallas Zoo has begun to build a 55-acre (22 ha) "Wilds of Africa," to be the first zoo exhibit anywhere to show every major habitat of a continent. The gorilla habitat takes the visitor along a rain-forest pathway and inside a thatched field research station from which the apes can be observed much as a field biologist would. The Brookfield Zoo in Chicago houses under one roof replicas of three rain forests — Asian, African and South American — accompanied by artificial thunder and rain. Tropical rain-forest replicas have been added to numerous zoos, and more are to come. These are sometimes called "immersion" exhibits. The visitor enters a new environment altogether, feels the humidity, hears the sounds of water, the calls of birds, the growl of a tiger long before catching a glimpse of them.

Such exhibits are not only more entertaining for a more sophisticated public but are more educational. This, they say, is pretty much how it is in a rain forest, or at a waterhole on the veld. More and more zoos are cooperating with local natural-history museums, to broaden their own exhibits with museum material and also to liven up museums with live animal displays. The Emen Zoo in north Holland is linked directly to two museums — one that tells the story of evolution by displaying live animals and fossils side by side, and a natural-history museum devoted to changing biological themes such as reproduction or the senses. Another entertainment/education device used by zoos, notably by the St. Louis Zoo, are the "interactive" exhibits employed by many science museums where computerized "games" designed to teach various biological concepts lead one along the path of learning.

In zoo after zoo, the message of these education programs is increasingly focused on conservation — endangered species and the loss of wildlife habitat. In a world of some 5 billion people, and soon to be twice that, it may seem a bit quixotic to educate some 250 million people (mostly already well educated and middle class) each year about the beauty and necessity of wildlife and the need to preserve it and its habitat. Certainly, education is not the only answer, but it can fairly be said that without this kind of understanding, there will be no solution to the problem. And it is precisely such an educated constituency that will help persuade governments, businesses and other funding sources to aid the expensive work that the revolutionary zoo of today is performing on behalf of genetic diversity.

That mankind is going to have to change a lot of expensive habits is rapidly becoming clear — not just from wildlife advocates and other environmentalists but from a complex series of events that we have unwittingly set in motion that may well bring about one of the fastest climatic shifts in the earth's history. This is, of course, the greenhouse effect — the rapid accumulation of gases in the atmosphere (especially carbon dioxide and methane) that let the sun's heat in but keep it from readily escaping. The tendency, thus, is for the earth to heat up, and some scientists say it has already begun. Few dispute that it will occur to some extent. A worst-case estimate has the average global temperature rising as much as five degrees in the next fifty years. Predictions suggest that the warming would be less drastic in the tropics — one or two degrees — and most severe in polar regions — a whopping twelve degrees.

An early effect would be the melting of the ice caps: it is only on polar ice floes that the polar bear, walrus and a variety of seals live. With the floes gone, such animals would have to live in zoos, and probably forever. And, of course, melting ice means higher sea levels. The level of the sea has risen about a foot (30 cm) globally in the past century for reasons that remain obscure, and beaches have been steadily eroding, marshlands filling with standing saltwater. Some greenhouse prognosticators say that a 5 foot (1.5 m) rise in fifty years is possible, far more than is needed to completely drown such places as Florida's subtropical wonderland, the Everglades, as well as virtually every coral reef in the world. (It is more than a natural-history oddity that alligator eggs that hatch at about 80°F [30°C] produce females, while those that hatch at about 93°F (34°C) produce males. The last wild alligators might consist of an entire geriatric generation of males.)

To truly predict the extent and the overall, much less regional, effects of global warming is, so far, beyond the largest computers' capacity, but a few ecologists have developed likely scenarios. Dry areas, such as the American Southwest, could become wetter. An odd result would be that more grass would grow, to densities that would support large brushfires in the dry months that would wipe out most cacti, which are not fire resistant and some of which serve as the exclusive home for certain animal species, for example, owls. In mountain areas, warm-weather zones would move up the slopes, forcing colder zones upward and, because mountains are basically cone-shaped, such zones would inevitable grow smaller, their wildlife diminishing in number and becoming subject to all the dangers inherent in small populations. Reserves set aside for certain species arrays would become unsuitable as their ecological systems changed. Planners have pointed out that wildlife could move away, toward cooler realms, if we were to supply corridors of natural habitat out of the reserves. But most such reserves are virtual islands, surrounded by the implacable barriers of human habitation and activity, and there is little reason to believe that ecosystems, such as forests, are capable of migrating as fast as they would have to. At the end of the Pleistocene, some 10,000 years ago, beech forests in the United States chased the receding ice northward at a rate of 12 miles (20 km) per century. It has been estimated that, if atmospheric carbon dioxide were to double in less than a century, beech forests would have to move 310 miles (500 km) in the same period to be in a suitable climate.

No one is truly expecting the worst-case scenario to come about. Presumably, we will find a way to ameliorate the effects of global warming by changing our habits. And, possibly, some of the measures taken to preserve the climate will also serve to alter some of the human activity that is eliminating wildlife habitat at today's alarming and growing rate. But that there will be a wave of extinctions in any event is certain. The loss of a few acres of tropical rain forest can eradicate untold numbers of insect species. Presently it is estimated that about 2,000 of the approximately 11,000 species of birds and mammals of the world are endangered in the wild. If all the world's zoos were to give themselves over exclusively to captive-breeding programs, they could still handle only some 800 species. Zoos aren't the only answer to this growing problem and no one is more aware of this than the people who work in them. But, it can fairly be said that, without zoos, there will be no solution. Zoos remain among the most crucial garrisons of life in a planetary war of attrition, a war the extent of which cannot be predicted but one for which future generations will hold us utterly responsible.

The Camel House has been a landmark in the London Zoo since the early days. This view was drawn by F. Hulme in 1848.

Appendix A: Major Zoos of the World

The publisher would like to thank the directors and staff of the many zoos who went out of their way to provide information for the list that appears below.

NOTES:
The statistics given below were specially solicited for this book and are up-to-date at the time of publication. Clearly, however, animal populations within zoos are changing constantly. The numbers should be understood as approximations only.

The ratio of species to specimens gives a rough notion of the emphasis placed by a particular zoo on breeding programs, as opposed to the older conception of the "postage stamp" zoo, in which individuals of as many species as possible are represented singly or in pairs.

In the case of many zoos listed, mention is made of studbooks maintained by the curatorial staff. While this may demonstrate a commitment to species preservation on the part of the studbook holders, the issue is somewhat complicated. Europe, North America and the Australasian countries operate separate species preservation plans, and within each plan, regional studbook holders are sometimes named. So, for instance, there is more than one gorilla studbook holder listed. This is a matter of logistics: it is easier to exchange breeding animals within a continent than globally. It should also be understood that the fact that a zoo holds no studbook does not necessarily indicate a lack of commitment to conservation.

Zoo publications are generally offered to members of the zoological societies that support the zoos. It is reasonable to assume, unless otherwise indicated, that such publications are written in the language of the country of origin. Where the address for zoo publications differs from that of the zoo itself, it is noted with the list of publications.

AUSTRALIA

Currumbin
Currumbin Sanctuary
28 Tomewin Street, Currumbin, Queensland 4223, Australia

The sanctuary encompasses 60 acres (24 ha) and receives about 420,000 visitors annually.

The collection concentrates on Australian fauna, particularly parrots, that are native to the region. It includes 24 species of mammals (377 specimens), 9 reptiles (19 specimens) and 127 birds (577 specimens).

Among the rare and endangered species bred within the sanctuary are bilby, Goodfellow's tree kangaroo, and Cloncurry and golden-shouldered parrots. Studbooks are in preparation for all species of black cockatoo and black-throated finch. The zoo is studbook holder for cassowary.

Healesville
Healesville Sanctuary
Badger Creek Road, Healesville, Victoria 3777, Australia

The sanctuary, which occupies 78 acres (31 ha), receives some 350,000 visitors annually.

Specializing in native Australian fauna, especially that indigenous to the southeast, Healesville Sanctuary maintains 42 species of mammals (476 specimens), 25 reptiles (98 specimens), 5 amphibians (13 specimens), 94 birds (736 specimens) and 6 fish (125 specimens).

Leadbeater's possum, mountain pygmy-possum and long-footed potoroo are among the threatened species bred at the sanctuary. Studbooks held include: brush-tailed rock wallaby, brush-tailed phascogale, eastern grass owl and superb lyrebird.

Melbourne
Royal Melbourne Zoological Gardens
PO Box 74, Parkville, Victoria 3052, Australia

Approximately 1 million people visit the 55-acre (22-ha) site annually.

The Melbourne Zoo, founded in 1857, is Australia's oldest. The collection includes 109 species of mammals (575 specimens), 77 reptiles (418 specimens), 7 amphibians (77 specimens), 168 birds (1,284 specimens) and 27 insecta (785 specimens). Among the notable features of the zoo is a walk-through butterfly house.

The Melbourne Zoo, with the Zoological Board of Victoria, administers the Australian Species Management Scheme. Many endangered species, particularly those indigenous to Australia, are bred at Melbourne. Among the notable successes was the

A birdwing butterfly on display at the Royal Melbourne Zoological Gardens.

conception by artificial insemination of a Mzuri, a gorilla, now five years old.

Zoo News, a newsletter, is offered quarterly to Friends of the Zoo.

Perth
Perth Zoo
PO Box 489, South Perth, Western Australia 6151, Australia

The Perth Zoo occupies a site of 48 acres (19 ha) and receives about 575,000 visitors annually.

The collection reflects an emphasis on primates and western Australian fauna. It includes 102 species of mammals (534 specimens), 45 reptiles (167 specimens), 3 amphibians (10 specimens), 145 birds (815 specimens) and 2 fish (2 specimens).

Among the rare and endangered species bred at the zoo are the numbat, western swamp turtle, western quoll, brush-tailed bettong, black-and-white ruffed lemurs, maned wolf, Persian leopard, Matschie's tree kangaroo, cotton-top tamarin and concolor gibbon. The zoo is regional studbook holder for the orangutan.

Sydney
Taronga Zoo
PO Box 20, Mosman, New South Wales 2088,
Australia

Approximately 1 million visitors tour Taronga's
70 acres (28 ha) each year.

The collection, emphasizing Australian fauna,
includes: 122 species of mammals (874 specimens),
127 reptiles (582 specimens), 4 amphibians
(16 specimens), 292 birds (1,644 specimens) and 161 fish
(552 specimens).

Among the rare and endangered species bred
successfully at the zoo are: red panda, platypus,
malleefowl, Lord Howe Island woodhen, bilby,
eastern grass owl. There are plans to return captive-
bred malleefowl and eastern grass owls to the wild.

AUSTRIA

Innsbruck
Alpenzoo Innsbruck-Tirol
Weiherburggasse 37, A-6020 Innsbruck, Austria

Approximately 300,000 visitors tour the 10 acre (4 ha)
zoo each year.

The Alpenzoo specializes in local fauna,
particularly those that are endangered or extinct
within the region. The collection includes 10 species
of mammals (81 specimens), 7 reptiles (24 specimens),
8 amphibians (104 specimens), 61 birds (163 specimens)
and 45 fish (532 specimens).

Breeding programs, some leading to release back
into the wild, are in place for bearded vulture, otter,
ibex, and peregrine falcon, among others.

A multilingual zoo guide is available to visitors. In
addition, several scientific papers relating to the
work of the zoo have been published.

BELGIUM

Antwerp
Royal Zoological Society of Antwerp
Koningin Astridplein 26, 2018 Antwerp, Belgium

The zoological society operates two zoos: the
Antwerp Zoo occupies 24 acres (10 ha) and receives
1.3 million visitors annually; the Planckendael Zoo,
96 acres (40 ha), receives 300,000 visitors.

The Antwerp zoos bring together a very large
collection of species: 205 mammals (1,118 specimens), 78 reptiles (286 specimens), 6 amphibians
(175 specimens), 439 birds (1,883 specimens) and
185 fish (1,857 specimens).

Also included in the Society's operations are a
spectacular botanical garden, delphinarium and
natural history museum. Active breeding programs
are in effect for okapi, babirusa, Congo peacock,
stork, otter, Indian rhinoceros and bonobo.
Studbooks are maintained by zoo staff for okapi,
Congo peacock and bonobo.

Publications include: *Zoo Antwerpen* (120 BF per
number); *Acta Zoologica et Pathologica Antverpiensia*
(250–500 BF, depending on number of pages).

Genk
Limburgse Zoo Zwartberg
Marcel Habetslaan 58, 3600 Zwartberg-Genk, Belgium

Situated on 50 acres (20 ha), the Limburg Zoo is seen
by 500,000 visitors annually.

In its collection are 149 species of mammals
(1,207 specimens), 20 reptiles (122 specimens),
12 amphibians (25 specimens), 56 birds (497 specimens), 120 fish (2,160 specimens) and 9 invertebrates
(260 specimens).

The zoo specializes in bear and wild cattle.
Successful breeding programs for many endangered
species are under way, including: polar bear, Père
David deer, wisent (European bison), white
rhinoceros, chimpanzee and kulan.

A zoo guide is available to visitors.

BERMUDA

Bermuda Aquarium, Natural History Museum
and Zoo
PO Box FL 145, Flatts, Bermuda, FL BX

Each year 135,000 people visit the 7 acre (3 ha) site of
the Bermuda Zoo.

The collection, which concentrates on island
species, includes 2 species of mammals (12 specimens),
9 reptiles (74 specimens), 44 birds (178 specimens) and
107 fish (861 specimens).

Caribbean flamingos and Galapagos tortoises have
been bred successfully at the Zoo.

A quarterly newsletter, *Crittertalk*, is sent to
members.

BRAZIL

Curitiba
Zoologico de Curitiba
Passaeio Publico-Administracao, 80030, Curitiba, PR,
Brazil

The Curitiba Zoo occupies 156 acres (63 ha) and the Central Zoo, 17 acres (7 ha). As admission is free, attendance has not been accurately calculated.

The collection, which emphasizes Brazilian mammals and birds, consists of: 48 species of mammals (409 specimens), 21 reptiles (204 specimens), 176 birds (1,103 specimens) and 20 fish (90 specimens).

Breeding programs for endangered species include maned wolf, giant anteater, Sumatran tiger (for all three of which the zoo maintains the studbook) and otter.

Rio Grande do Sul
Parque Zoologico da Fundacao Zoobotanica do Rio Grande do Sul BR-116, Parada 41, Caixa Postal 36, 93200 Sapucaia do Sul, Rio Grande do Sul, Brazil

More than 450,000 people visit the zoo annually. It occupies 383 acres (153 ha).

In the collection, which concentrates on Brazilian fauna, are: 68 species of mammals (436 specimens), 12 reptiles (104 specimens) and 136 birds (1,619 specimens).

Breeding programs devoted to endangered species include those for: maned wolf, king vulture, tapir, caiman, spectacled bear and pacarana.

CANADA

Calgary
Calgary Zoo, Botanical Garden and Prehistoric Park
PO Box 3036, Station B, Calgary, Alberta T2M 4R8, Canada

The Calgary Zoo and its associated park and botanical gardens are situated on an island in the Bow River. It occupies 439 acres (176 ha) and is visited by 783,000 people annually.

The collection focuses on northern fauna and includes: 90 species of mammals (410 specimens), 44 reptiles (116 specimens), 12 amphibians (60 specimens), 148 birds (519 specimens) and 15 fish (231 specimens).

The Calgary Zoo is active in thirteen SSP programs under the auspices of the AAZPA. Staff maintain studbooks for wood bison, alpine ibex and swift fox.

A quarterly newsletter, *Dinny's Digest*, is distributed to members of the Calgary Zoological Society.

Cambridge
African Lion Safari
RR 1, Cambridge, Ontario N1R 5S2, Canada

Some 450,000 visitors drive through the 275-acre (110-ha) park annually.

The collection includes 55 species of mammals (602 specimens) and 83 birds (420 specimens).

Cheetah and white rhinoceros have been bred successfully.

Charlesbourg
Jardin zoologique du Québec
8191 avenue du Zoo, Charlesbourg, Québec G1G 4G4, Canada

The zoo, which in summer months includes La Petite Ferme for children and an insect zoo, occupies 58 acres (23 ha) north of Quebec City. It receives some 225,000 visitors annually.

In the collection there are: 54 species of mammals (212 specimens) and 156 species of birds (501 specimens). There is some emphasis on big cats and primates.

The Quebec Zoo breeds eastern bluebird, Siberian tiger and lemur.

Les Carnets de zoologie, a quarterly magazine, is published by the Société zoologique de Québec, 9141 avenue du Zoo, Charlesbourg, Québec, G1G 4G4.

Holyrood
Salmonier Nature Park
PO Box 190, Holyrood, Newfoundland A0A 2R0, Canada

The Nature Park, situated on 3,000 acres (1200 ha) of which 100 acres (40 ha) have been developed, receives 30,000 visitors annually.

Salmonier keeps only those species indigenous to Newfoundland and Labrador: 10 species of mammals (20 specimens), 2 reptiles (2 specimens), 5 amphibians (20 specimens), 10 birds (30 specimens) and 3 fish (8 specimens).

The Park has a breeding program for arctic hare.

Two summer newsletters are distributed free to visitors.

Montreal
Jardin zoologique de Montréal
3400 boulevard des Trinitaires, Montréal, Québec H4E 4J3, Canada

Approximately 350,000 people visit the 30,000 square foot (10 000 square metre) zoo each year.

The specialty is birds. The collection includes 7 species of mammals (68 specimens), 3 reptiles (3 specimens) and 60 birds (132 specimens).

Toronto
Metropolitan Toronto Zoo
PO Box 280, West Hill, Ontario M1S 3A1, Canada

The Toronto Zoo occupies 710 acres (284 ha) in the eastern suburbs of the city. About 1.4 million visitors tour the zoo in a year.

The collection, arranged zoogeographically, includes: 106 species of mammals (1,002 specimens), 51 reptiles (229 specimens), 16 amphibians (167 specimens), 144 birds (622 specimens), 117 fish (1,538 specimens) and 83 invertebrates (number of specimens not supplied).

The Toronto Zoo is actively engaged in breeding endangered species and in associated research. One current project, for example, concentrates on the possibility of artificial propagation of endangered cat species.

A newsletter and guidebook are supplied to members of the zoological society.

Making a virtue of necessity, the Metropolitan Toronto Zoo opens its trails to cross-country skiers in the winter months.

Vancouver
Stanley Park Zoological Gardens
2099 Beach Avenue, Vancouver, British Columbia
V7V 2V7, Canada

The Stanley Park Zoo occupies 21 acres (8 ha) and receives some 1.2 million visitors a year.

The collection presently consists of: 20 species of mammals (79 specimens), 11 reptiles (44 specimens) and 58 birds (213 specimens).

The newly created Stanley Park Zoological Society is overseeing redevelopment plans for the zoo that will concentrate efforts on displaying and conserving native species. The zoo is presently involved in the SSP program for the Humboldt penguin.

Vancouver Aquarium
PO Box 3232, Vancouver, British Columbia V6B 3X8, Canada

The aquarium occupies a site of 1.2 acres (.5 ha) and receives approximately 950,000 visitors in a year.

The Vancouver Aquarium's collection concentrates on marine mammals, fish and invertebrates of the Pacific Ocean and Amazon River. It includes: 7 species of mammals (25 specimens), 22 reptiles (87 specimens), 19 amphibians (101 specimens), 19 birds (46 specimens) and 503 fish (8,407 specimens).

Breeding programs are in place for killer whale, sea otter, Amazonian birds and many fish, including sculpin, wolfeel and cichlid.

A quarterly newsletter, *Seapen*, and journal, *Waters*, are sent to members.

Winnipeg
Assiniboine Park Zoo
2355 Corydon Avenue, Winnipeg, Manitoba R3P 0R5, Canada

Situated on 100 acres (40 ha), the zoo receives 670,000 visitors a year.

The Assiniboine Zoo specializes in animals of the Holarctic region, but also features a significant number of exotic soft-billed birds and endangered primates. It includes 75 species of mammals (450 specimens), 8 reptiles (15 specimens), 2 amphibians (12 specimens) and 145 birds (620 specimens).

Among the endangered species bred at the zoo are: vicuna, lion-tailed macaque, bushdog and grey gibbon.

A zoo guide is offered for sale at the zoo. *Zoolog*, the zoological society newsletter, is sent to members only.

CHILE

Santiago
Jardin Zoologico Nacional
PIO Nono 450, Santiago, Chile

Approximately 700,000 visitors tour the 18-acre (7-ha) Santiago Zoo each year.

The collection, which emphasizes Chilean Fauna, includes: 52 species of mammals (381 specimens), 9 reptiles (35 specimens) and 106 birds (851 specimens).

Breeding programs are in place for, among other threatened species, Andean condor and Chilean pudu.

CZECHOSLOVAKIA

Ostrava
Zoologická zahrada Ostrava
7100 00, Ostrava 2, Stromovka, Czechoslovakia

More than 400,000 people visit the 260-acre (104-ha) Ostrava Zoo each year.

The collection emphasizes Eurasian fauna, particularly deer, large cats and waterfowl. It includes 73 species of mammals (328 specimens), 9 reptiles (15 specimens) and 100 birds (724 specimens).

The zoo breeds a number of endangered species, including: Thamin deer, rare tigers, lion-tailed macaque, Kulan wild ass and Andean condor.

DENMARK

Copenhagen
Copenhagen Zoo
Sdr. Fasanvej 79, DK 2000 Frederiksberg, Denmark

The Copenhagen Zoo occupies a site 27 acres (11 ha) in extent. There are just over 1 million visitors annually.

In the collection there are: 78 species of mammals (669 specimens), 57 reptiles (277 specimens), 18 amphibians (106 specimens), 129 birds (550 specimens) and 18 fish and invertebrates (400 specimens).

Among the zoo's recent innovations are the Ape Jungle, Arctic World, and Children's Zoo with Biological Playground. There are breeding programs in place for some twenty endangered species, including notably Asian elephant and musk ox. The studbook for muskox is maintained at the zoo.

Publications include a quarterly newsletter, guidebook and annual report.

The elephant house at the Copenhagen Zoo, about 1905. The bull elephant on the left was called Chang, and his mate was called Ellen. They produced offspring in 1908, 1912 and 1916.

FRANCE

Paris
Parc zoologique de Paris
53 avenue de Saint-Maurice, 75012, Paris, France

The Paris Zoo is located on 38 acres (15 ha) and receives some 950,000 visitors annually.

The collection is general. It includes 110 species of mammals (460 specimens) and 145 species of birds (665 specimens).

Among rare and endangered species bred in the zoo is the cheetah. The studbook for Eld's deer is maintained by staff of the zoo.

FEDERAL REPUBLIC OF GERMANY

Berlin
Zoologischer Garten Berlin
Hardenbergplatz 8, 1000 Berlin 30,
Federal Republic of Germany

The Berlin Zoo occupies 84 acres (34 ha) and receives nearly 3 million visitors annually.

Its collection is among the largest in the world. It includes 276 species of mammals (1,563 specimens), 96 reptiles (314 specimens), 39 amphibians (346 specimens), 647 birds (2,936 specimens), 431 fish (3,433 specimens) and 223 invertebrates (6,000 specimens).

The breeding programs embrace a multitude of species. Among mammals, the zoo is especially concerned with primates, carnivores and ungulates and, among birds, with parrots, cranes, ducks and geese. Studbooks for African rhinoceros, gaur and pampas deer are maintained at the zoo.

A guidebook (available in German and English editions) and *BONGO* (annual report and scientific reports) are published by the zoo.

The aquarium at the Berlin Zoo, showing the "Crocodile Beach" in the foreground, about 1914.

Cologne
Zoologischer Garten Köln
Riehler Strasse 173, D-5000 Köln 60, Federal Republic
of Germany

The Cologne zoo and aquarium occupy 49 acres
(20 ha) and receive 1.5 million visitors annually.

The collection contains: 94 species of mammals
(635 specimens), 77 reptiles (486 specimens), 16 amphibians (326 specimens), 117 birds (830 specimens)
and 216 fish (2,675 specimens).

Primates have been an area of particular specialization. Zoo staff are fostering breeding programs
for many species, notably Przewalski's horse, ruffed
lemur and douc langur.

Zeitschrift des Kölner Zoo is available for 20 DM
per year.

Frankfurt
Frankfurt Zoological Gardens
Alfred-Brehm-Platz 16, D-6000 Frankfurt am Main 1,
Federal Republic of Germany

The Frankfurt Zoo and Exotarium (which houses
reptiles and an aquarium) occupies a 27-acre (11-ha)
site and receives about 2.5 million visitors annually.

The diverse collection includes: 122 species of
mammals (1,188 specimens), 58 reptiles (265 specimens), 21 amphibians (309 specimens), 175 birds
(703 specimens), 245 fish (2,675 specimens) and
56 invertebrates (509 specimens)

Breeding programs encompass many endangered
species. Zoo staff maintain studbooks for gorilla,
maned wolf, bush dog and black-footed cat.

Zoo and aquarium guidebook, and a special guidebook for children are offered for sale to the public.
These guides are among the best offered at any zoo.

Hanover
Zoologischer Garten Hannover
Adenauerallee 3, D-3000 Hannover 1, Federal Republic
of Germany

Approximately 800,000 visitors annually tour the
53-acre (21-ha) Hanover Zoo.

There are 124 species of mammals (635 specimens)
in the collection, 18 reptiles (140 specimens) and
125 birds (536 specimens).

The zoo is particularly strong in its collection of
antelope and primates, and notable for its Asian
elephants and walrus. It maintains the mandrill
studbook.

A zoo magazine, *Der Zoofreund*, is issued to
members.

Munich
Munchener Tierpark Hellabrunn AG
Tierparkstrasse 30, D-8000 Munchen 90, Federal
Republic of Germany

The Munich Zoo is situated on 90 acres (36 ha).
About 1.4 million people visit it annually.

The large collection is general, but emphasizes
endangered species. It includes 101 species of
mammals (731 specimens), 38 reptiles (125 specimens),
120 birds (806 specimens) and 88 fish (1,492 specimens).

Among the rare and threatened animals that are
bred successfully at the zoo are Przewalski's horse,
Mhorr gazelle, muskox, silver gibbon, gaur, kiang,
snow goat, giant anteater, wood bison, maned wolf
and red ibis. The Munich Zoo is studbook holder for
the black stork.

Stuttgart
Wilhelma, Zoologisch-Botanischer Garten
Postfach 50 12 27, Neckartalstrasse, D-7000, Stuttgart
50, Federal Republic of Germany.

The Stuttgart Zoo occupies 60 acres (24 ha) and is
seen by 1.7 million visitors a year.

The collection, especially strong in great apes and
coral reef fish, includes: 126 species of mammals
(841 specimens), 89 reptiles (330 specimens), 30 amphibians (231 specimens), 200 birds (753 specimens),
414 fish (5,547 specimens) and 148 invertebrates
(1,321 specimens).

The zoo is involved in a number of breeding
programs involving endangered species. It is
studbook holder for the babirusa.

The elephants in the Dresden Zoo photographed by
William Mann sometime in the 1930s.

GREAT BRITAIN

Chessington
Chessington World of Adventures
Chessington, Surrey KT9 2NE, Great Britain

The Chessington Zoo occupies 130 acres (53 ha) and receives more than 1 million visitors annually.

The collection includes: 50 species of mammals (145 specimens), 27 reptiles (82 specimens), 7 amphibians (14 specimens) and 60 birds (196 specimens).

Chessington breeds a number of endangered species — especially primates — successfully, among them: ocelot, snow leopard, gorilla, Diana monkey, ring-tailed lemur, ruffed lemur, Barbary ape, Celebese black ape, hippopotamus, jaguar, puma, ibis, scarlet ibis, and a variety of macaws and parrots.

Edinburgh
Edinburgh Zoo and Highland Wildlife Park
Royal Zoological Society of Scotland, Murrayfield, Edinburgh EH12 6TS, Scotland

The Edinburgh Zoo occupies 85 acres (34 ha) and receives some 532,000 visitors annually. The Highland Wildlife Park, also operated by the Royal Zoological Society of Scotland, is located in Kingussie, Inverness-shire, where it occupies 250 acres (100 ha) and receives about 92,000 visitors.

The Edinburgh Zoo's collection is a general one, with some emphasis on penguins and primates, particularly chimpanzee, gorilla and guenon. It houses 66 species of mammals (325 specimens), 29 reptiles (193 specimens), 9 amphibians (423 specimens) and 70 birds (368 specimens). The Highland Wildlife Park emphasizes highland species. It keeps 24 species of mammals (202 specimens) and 39 birds (157 specimens).

The society is actively engaged in breeding endangered species. Both zoos issue a guidebook, and a quarterly newsletter is sent to members.

Jersey
Jersey Wildlife Preservation Trust
Les Augres Manor, Trinity, Jersey, Channel Islands

The Jersey Zoo occupies 26 acres (10 ha) and receives in excess of 300,000 visitors annually.

In the collection of animals are 28 species of mammals (279 specimens), 27 reptiles (329 specimens), 4 amphibians (114 specimens) and 38 birds (446 specimens).

The emphasis from the zoo's inception has been on building breeding groups of endangered species

— roughly 80 percent of the species represented are threatened or endangered — and on training staff to manage such programs. The Trust sponsors research and conservation projects in the Mascarenes Islands, Madagascar, Brazil, Mexico, St. Lucia, St. Vincent and Jamaica. Studbooks for golden lion tamarin, Goeldi's

The London Zoo, Regent's Park.

monkey, gorilla and thick-billed parrot are maintained by zoo staff.

Dodo Journal and *Dodo Dispatch* are available to members of the Jersey Wildlife Trust. For other publications, see *A Jubilee Bibliography*, available from the Trust.

London
London Zoo and Whipsnade Park
Zoological Society of London, Regent's Park, London NW1 4RY, Great Britain.

The London Zoo occupies 36 acres (14 ha) in Regent's Park and receives 1.3 million visitors a year. Whipsnade, also run by the Zoological Society of London, occupies 580 acres (232 ha) in the county of Bedfordshire, and receives 450,000 visitors.

This is one of the largest collections of animals maintained by any zoo. London: 163 species of mammals (1,403 specimens), 106 reptiles (403 specimens), 34 amphibians (169 specimens), 302 birds (994 specimens), 240 fish (2,300 specimens) and 112 invertebrates (3,600 specimens). Whipsnade: 64 species of mammals (1,225 specimens), 11 reptiles (86 specimens), 2 amphibians (6 specimens), 94 birds (922 specimens), 18 fish (80 specimens) and 24 invertebrates (55 specimens).

The Zoological Society has, from its inception, been concerned with scientific work and continues to maintain extensive research facilities in the areas of veterinary science, reproduction, nutrition and genetics. In addition, the society supports many overseas conservation and research projects. Over 100 endangered or vulnerable species are involved in the zoo's many breeding programs.

In addition to the zoo guides, the Zoological Society publishes the *Journal of Zoology*, *Transactions* and *Symposia of the Zoological Society of London*, and the *International Zoo Yearbook*.

Warminster
Lions of Longleat Safari Park
Warminster, Wiltshire BA12 7NJ, Great Britain

Approximately 400,000 visitors tour the park's 300 acres (120 ha) annually.

The collection includes 27 species of mammals (310 specimens), 3 reptiles (6 specimens) and 10 birds (38 specimens).

White rhinoceros, Bengal tiger, Rothschild giraffe, California sealion and Père David deer have been bred successfully in the park.

Windsor
Windsor Safari Park
Winkfield Road, Windsor, Berkshire SL4 4AY, Great Britain

The park occupies 140 acres (56 ha). It receives 950,000 visitors a year.

The collection includes 30 species of mammals

(290 specimens), 8 reptiles (18 specimens), 1 amphibian (3 specimens), 20 birds (120 specimens) and 3 fish (15 specimens).

Cheetah, golden lion tamarin, white rhinoceros and African elephant are among the endangered species successfully bred in the park.

Woburn
Woburn Wild Animal Kingdom

Woburn Park, Woburn, Bedfordshire MK17 9QN, Great Britain

Some 400,000 visitors tour the 350 acres (140 ha) of the park each year.

The collection includes: 26 species of mammals (267 specimens), 1 amphibian (6 specimens) and 11 birds (112 specimens).

Asian elephants, bongo and Przewalski's horse are bred at the park.

The Budapest Zoo in the 1930s.

HUNGARY

Budapest
Zoological and Botanical Garden of the City of
Budapest
Budapest XIV., Allatkerti krt. 6., Budapest 5, Pf. 469.
1371, Hungary

The venerable and beautiful Budapest Zoo occupies a
33-acre (13-ha) site and receives about 1.4 million
visitors each year.

The Budapest Zoo's collection includes: 123 species
of mammals (455 specimens), 47 reptiles (128 specimens), 11 amphibians (61 specimens), 155 birds
(769 specimens) and 100 fish (1,067 specimens).

A number of endangered species are bred at the
zoo, notably gorilla, Siberian tiger, black gibbon and
bettong.

INDIA

Calcutta
Zoological Garden
Allipore, Calcutta 700027, India

The 50-acre (20-ha) zoo receives 2.4 million visitors
a year.

The collection is a general one, embracing both
exotic and indigenous animals. It includes 62 species
of mammals (474 specimens), 23 reptiles (70 specimens), 140 birds (1,659 specimens) and 94 fish
(1,054 specimens).

Bengal tiger, Indian one-horned rhinoceros and
brow-antlered deer, all endangered, have been
successfully bred at the zoo.

New Delhi
National Zoological Park, Delhi
1 Mathura Road, New Delhi 110003, India

About 1.6 million people visit the Delhi Zoo
annually. It is situated on 186 acres (74 ha).

The collection concentrates particularly on
endangered mammals of the Indian subcontinent.
It includes 68 species of mammals (374 specimens),
5 reptiles (27 specimens) and 97 birds (1,210 specimens).

A number of endangered species have been bred
successfully, including lion-tailed macaque, Thamin
deer, white tiger, wild ass and Indian and black
rhinoceroses. The zoo maintains studbooks for white
tiger and Thamin deer.

Publications of the zoo include a bulletin, guide
book and zoo history.

IRELAND

Dublin
Royal Zoological Society of Ireland
Phoenix Park, Dublin 8, Ireland

The Dublin Zoo is situated on 30 acres (12 ha) and is
visited by roughly 500,000 people annually. It also
maintains a separate branch at Fota Island.

Within the collection are 70 species of mammals
(266 specimens), 13 reptiles (44 specimens) and
102 birds (461 specimens).

The zoo is active with British and European zoos
in a number of breeding programs. Particularly
notable is the breeding group of cheetahs.

ISRAEL

Haifa
Haifa Biological Institute and Educational Zoo
124 Hatishbi Street, Haifa 34455, Israel

Each year 150,000 people visit the zoo's 5-acre (2-ha)
facility.

The Haifa Institute, which specializes in reptiles,
maintains 37 species of mammals (160 specimens), 69
reptiles (187 specimens) and 44 birds (227 specimens).

Some educational materials are published for use
in Israeli schools.

ITALY

Rome
Zoological Garden of Rome
Viale Giardino Zoologico, 20, Rome 00197, Italy

The Rome Zoo occupies 41 acres (17 ha) and receives
approximately 500,000 visitors each year.

The collection, a general one, includes: 116 species
of mammals (509 specimens), 48 reptiles (196
specimens), 1 amphibian (1 specimen) and 114 birds
(439 specimens).

Many endangered species are the focus of
breeding programs at the zoo. Staff keep studbooks
for: gorilla, orangutan, cheetah, Grevy's zebra, pigmy
hippopotamus and black rhinoceros.

JAPAN

Nagoya
Nagoya Higashiyama Zoo
3-70 Higashiyamamotomachi, Chikusaku, Nagoya 464,
Japan

The zoo, situated on 83 acres (33 ha), receives approximately 300,000 visitors annually.

The collection, notable for its koalas and large cats, includes: 107 species of mammals (469 specimens), 23 reptiles (63 specimens), 20 amphibians (179 specimens), 92 birds (347 specimens) and 217 fish (2,046 specimens).

The Nagoya Zoo is active in breeding many endangered species. It keeps seventeen international and sixteen domestic studbooks.

A quarterly newsletter is issued to members of the Zoo.

Tokyo
Ueno Zoological Gardens
Ueno Park, Taito-ku, Tokyo 110, Japan

The 35-acre (14-ha) Ueno Zoo receives more than 6 million visitors a year.

The collection includes: 79 species of mammals (342 specimens), 82 reptiles (271 specimens), 28 amphibians (204 specimens), 196 birds (653 specimens) and 76 fish (982 specimens).

Now more than 100 years old (it was founded in 1882), the Ueno Zoo is increasingly involved in breeding endangered species. A notable achievement has been the successful conception, by artificial insemination, and subsequent rearing of two giant pandas. The zoo holds the studbook for the red-crowned crane.

A zoo guide and picture book are offered for sale by the Tokyo Zoological Park Society.

NEW ZEALAND

Auckland
Auckland Zoological Park
Motions Road, Western Springs, Auckland 2, New Zealand

The Auckland Zoo occupies 42 acres (17 ha) and receives 594,000 visitors annually.

Like most antipodean zoos, the Auckland Zoo specializes in native fauna. It currently keeps 47 species of mammals (275 specimens), 79 reptiles (509 specimens), 27 amphibians (220 specimens), 3 birds (27 specimens) and 33 fish (216 specimens).

Active breeding programs involve North Island kiwi, North Island brown kiwi, tuatara and Antipodes Island parakeet.

A club newsletter is distributed to members of the zoo.

Wellington
Wellington Zoological Gardens
Newtown Park, Wellington 2, New Zealand

The Wellington Zoo occupies 30 acres (12 ha) and receives close to 200,000 visitors in a year.

The collection, emphasizing endangered exotic animals and native fauna, includes: 36 species of mammals (151 specimens), 7 reptiles (41 specimens), 2 amphibians (8 specimens), 67 birds (336 specimens) and 30 fish (126 specimens).

The staff keep the studbook for the brown kiwi. Among the endangered species that are bred at the zoo are the tuatara, New Zealand brown teal, Antipodes Island parakeet, snow leopard, Siberian tiger, black-and-white ruffed lemurs, sitatunga, chimpanzee and agile gibbon.

NORWAY

Bergen
Bergen Aquarium
Nordnesparken 2, N5005 Bergen, Norway

The aquarium, which occupies a site of approximately 22,500 square feet (2100 square metres), receives some 165,000 visitors annually.

The animal collection, emphasizing the marine fauna of the Norwegian coast, includes: 3 species of mammals (8 specimens), 2 amphibians (12 specimens), 3 birds (22 specimens), 83 fish (approx. 1,000 specimens) and 200 invertebrates (approx. 1,500).

Active breeding programs involve the grey seal and common or harbor seal.

Publications of the aquarium include an annual report and multilingual guidebook.

PERU

Lima
Zoologico del Parque de las Leyendas
Av. La Marina, S/N Cuadra 24, Lima 32, Peru

The Lima Zoo receives approximately 1.4 million visitors annually. It is 150 acres (60 ha) in extent.

The collection, which emphasizes fauna of South America, particularly animals indigenous to Peru, is displayed in simulations of three ecological zones: coast, mountain and tropical forest. It includes: 42 species of mammals (416 specimens), 15 reptiles (180 specimens), 1 amphibian (3 specimens), 56 birds (290 specimens) and 15 fish (150 specimens).

According to the article that accompanied this illustration in *Harper's Weekly*, in May 1874, the Zoological Society of London paid £4,000 for this "Javan" rhinoceros — a hefty sum.

POLAND

Warsaw
Miejski Ogrod Zoologiczny
03-461 Warszawa, ul. Ratuszowa, Poland

More than 700,000 visitors tour the 100-acre (40-ha) grounds of the Warsaw Zoo each year.

The collection, which features South American fauna, includes 87 species of mammals (630 specimens), 34 reptiles (153 specimens), 2 amphibians (21 specimens), 84 birds (315 specimens) and 49 fish (1,490 specimens).

Among many endangered species bred at the zoo are Przewalski's horse and European bison.

SPAIN

Barcelona
Parc Zoologic de Barcelona
Parc de la Ciutadella, s/n, 08003 Barcelon, Spain

Roughly 1 million people tour the 30-acre (12-ha) zoo each year.

The Barcelona zoo houses 111 species of mammals (533 specimens), 93 reptiles (498 specimens), 11 amphibians (60 specimens), 184 birds (1,006 specimens) and 92 fish (5,102 specimens).

Areas of specialization include primates, aquatic mammals and birds indigenous to Spain. The zoo collaborates in a number of breeding programs with other European zoos.

Zoo Club, a quarterly magazine, is issued four times a year at an annual cost of 800 pesos.

SWEDEN

Stockholm
Skansen Foundation and Skansen-Akvariet
S-115 21 Stockholm, Sweden

The Skansen Foundation Zoo and Skansen-Akvariet occupy approximately 20 acres (8 ha). Skansen-Akvariet receives some 500,000, and the zoo 1.68 million visitors annually.

Skansen-Akvariet, specializing in breeding small primates and reptiles, keeps: 54 species of mammals (320 specimens), 38 reptiles (191 specimens), 12 amphibians (300 specimens), 4 birds (16 specimens) and 200 fish (2,000 specimens). Skansen Foundation Zoo, specializing in Nordic fauna, keeps: 28 species of mammals (154 specimens), 3 reptiles (15 specimens) and 38 birds (220 specimens).

Both Skansen-Akvariet and the zoo, under the auspices of the Skansen Foundation, are actively breeding endangered species, among them: golden lion tamarin, ruffed lemur, tamarin, marmoset and Cuban crocodile. Zoo staff maintain the studbook for wolves of Fenno-Scandinavian origin.

SWITZERLAND

Basel
Basel Zoological Gardens
4054 Basel, Birsigstrasse, Basel, Switzerland

One of the world's preeminent zoos, the Basel Zoo occupies just 35 acres (14 ha) and is visited by nearly 1 million visitors each year.

The collection includes 69 species of mammals (479 specimens), 38 reptiles (258 specimens), 7 amphibians (63 specimens), 126 birds (760 specimens) and 248 fish (2,757 specimens).

The Basel Zoo is known particularly for its work with Indian rhinoceros, gorilla, African elephant, Somali wild ass, snow leopard and California sealion. It is studbook holder for the Indian rhinoceros and pygmy hippopotamus.

Two zoo bulletins are sent to Friends of the Basel Zoo each year.

UNION OF SOVIET SOCIALIST REPUBLICS

Moscow
Moscow Zoo
B. Gruzinskaya 1, 123242 Moscow, USSR

More than 3 million visitors tour the Moscow Zoo's 45-acre (18-ha) site each year.

The large collection includes 115 species of mammals (589 specimens), 135 reptiles (370 specimens), 29 amphibians (223 specimens), 270 birds (1,459 specimens), 244 fish (2,080 specimens) and 6 invertebrates (121 specimens).

A number of strong areas can be identified: among mammals, large cats are well represented, particularly snow leopard, Pallas cat, cheetah; among birds, crane, pheasant, birds of prey and waterfowl are prominent. The zoo is also notable for its pit vipers, land turtles and dwarf false sturgeon.

The Moscow Zoo breeds many endangered species, including spectacled bear, Przewalski's horse and bearded vulture, and has had some success returning captive-bred species to the wild.

UNITED STATES OF AMERICA

Chicago
Chicago Zoological Park (Brookfield Zoo)
3300 Golf Road, Brookfield, Illinois 60513, USA
Telephone: (312) 485-0263

One of the major American zoos, the Brookfield Zoo occupies 200 acres (80 ha) and receives just under 2 million visitors annually.

One of the more remarkable displays at the Brookfield Zoo is Tropic World, where the rain forests of three regions — Asia, South America and Africa — are simulated in separate exhibits that include not only the flora and fauna, but also the weather: artificial thunderstorms occur at regular intervals.

Brookfield's collection includes: 153 species of mammals (1,340 specimens), 119 reptiles (237 specimens), 13 amphibians (36 specimens), 125 birds (515 specimens), 8 fish (15 specimens) and 8 invertebrates (57 specimens).

Among the breeding programs that involve SSP-listed animals are those for golden lion tamarin, lowland gorilla, orangutan, small-clawed otter, Siberian tiger, snow leopard, Indian elephant, Grevy's zebra, Przewalski's horse, black rhinoceros, okapi, Humboldt penguin and Rothschild's or Bali mynah.

A quarterly, *Preview*, is available for members of the Chicago Zoological Society and animal adoptive parents.

Chicago
Lincoln Park Zoological Gardens
2200 North Cannon Drive, Chicago, Illinois 60614, USA
Telephone: (312) 294-4662

The Lincoln Park Zoo occupies 35 acres (14 ha) and receives 4.5 million visitors annually.

The collection includes: 132 mammal species (737 specimens), 130 reptiles (364 specimens), 21 amphibians (57 specimens) and 136 birds (587 specimens).

Areas of special interest include: great apes, small mammals, perching birds and tortoises. The Lincoln Park Zoo is actively engaged in many breeding programs, among them: radiated tortoise, Dumeril's ground boa, Humboldt penguin, Bali mynah, Andean condor, several species of lemur, big cats including snow leopard, Siberian and Bengal tigers, Grevy's zebra and Arabian oryx. Staff at the zoo maintain the studbook for the spectacled bear.

The Lincoln Park Zoo Review, a quarterly, is available with membership in the Lincoln Park Zoological Society at the above address, or phone (312) 935-6700.

Cincinnati
Cincinnati Zoological and Botanical Gardens
3400 Vine Street, Cincinnati, Ohio 45220, USA
Telephone: (513) 281-4701

The Cincinnati Zoo occupies 64 acres (26 ha) and receives 1.3 million visitors annually.

The collection includes: 136 species of mammals (654 specimens), 111 reptiles (342 specimens), 55 am-

The Lion House, Bronx Zoo, 1905. Enlightened zoo design in the early years of the present century emphasized cleanliness and light. The zoo-goer's desire for an uninterrupted view of the animals was also a prime consideration. Zoos brought a bit of the wild to civilized places. With so much of the real wild still remaining, it would have made little sense in 1905 to have attempted a re-creation of the wild in the city.

phibians (215 specimens), 203 birds (800 specimens) and 74 fish (248 specimens).

The zoo built an insectarium — Insect World — at a cost of over $1 million (US) to display such rarities as the Madagascar hissing cockroach. It is one of two comparable displays in the United States; the other is in the National Zoo, Washington.

The Cincinnati Zoo has a particular interest in the lowland gorilla, white tiger, Sumatran rhinoceros, giant eland, king cheetah and okapi. Breeding programs have been initiated for many endangered species. The studbook for the black rhinoceros is kept at the zoo.

Zoonews, a newsletter, is distributed to members of the zoological society.

Dallas
Dallas Zoo
621 East Clarendon, Dallas, Texas 75203, USA
Telephone: (214) 670-6825

The Dallas Zoo receives about 500,000 visitors annually. Recently expanded, it now occupies 100 acres (40 ha).

The new Wilds of Africa exhibit features naturalistic habitats that can be viewed from a monorail or walking trail. The collection includes: 61 species of mammals (289 specimens), 119 reptiles (581 specimens), 9 amphibians (36 specimens) and 143 birds (576 specimens).

The zoo is engaged in a number of significant breeding programs. Especially notable are those for okapi, gorilla, many reptile and small antelope species and birds such as Congo peacock, Bali mynah, Andean condor, bald eagle, Nene goose and thick-billed parrot. Zoo staff maintain the studbook for Abyssinian ground hornbill and Stanley crane.

A newsletter is sent to members of the Dallas Zoological Society and participants in the Adopt-an-Animal program. For information about the Zoological Society, telephone: (214) 943-2771.

Houston
Houston Zoological Gardens
1513 Outer Belt Drive, Houston, Texas 77030, USA
Telephone: (713) 525-3300

Each year 1.7 million visitors tour the Houston Zoo's 55 acres (22 ha).

The collection includes 138 species of mammals (433 specimens), 178 reptiles (659 specimens), 22 amphibians (91 specimens), 182 birds (800 specimens) and 256 fish (650 specimens).

At Houston, the emphasis is on educational programs and on the preservation of endangered species, particularly birds. The zoo is SSP co-ordinator for the Micronesian kingfisher, and active in breeding the Lady Ross's turaco and violaceous turaco. Zoo staff keep the studbook for the Aruba Island rattlesnake.

Publications of the Zoological Society of Houston include a number of zoo guides and a member's journal.

Kansas City
Kansas City Zoo
6700 Zoo Drive, Kansas City, Missouri 64132, USA
Telephone: (816) 333-7406

The zoo presently occupies 80 acres (32 ha), however plans call for expansion to approximately 350 acres (142 ha). Annual attendance is in excess of 500,000 people.

The collection, a general one, includes: 48 species of mammals (226 specimens), 15 reptiles (25 specimens), 2 amphibians (7 specimens), 93 birds (306 specimens) and 8 fish (20 specimens).

Among the many endangered species for which breeding programs have been launched at Kansas City are: orangutan, kulan, guam rail, Micronesian kingfisher, Bali mynah and red panda.

Zoomin' magazine and *Friends of the Zoo* newsletter are available on subscription to members of Friends of the Zoo.

Los Angeles
Los Angeles Zoo
5333 Zoo Drive, Los Angeles, California 90027, USA
Telephone: (213) 666-4650

Each year, almost 2 million people visit the 113 acres (45 ha) occupied by the zoo.

The collection is a general one, with some emphasis on endangered species. It includes 139 species of mammals (749 specimens), 140 reptiles (506 specimens), 7 amphibians (15 specimens), 185 birds (722 specimens) and 1 fish (85 specimens).

The Los Angeles Zoo is actively involved in a number of SSP breeding programs. It holds the studbooks for mandrill, Andean condor, California condor and Indian and Sumatran rhinoceros.

Zooview, a quarterly magazine, and *GLAZANews*, a monthly newsletter, are available with membership in the Greater Los Angeles Zoo Association at the above address, or phone (213) 664-1100.

The Bear Pit at the London Zoo in 1835, by George Scharf. It remained the custom to put bears in holes in the ground, and to give people — if not dogs — the opportunity to bait them, for much of the nineteenth century.

Louisville
Louisville Zoological Garden
1100 Trevilian Way, PO Box 37250, Louisville, Kentucky
40233, USA
Telephone: (502) 459-2181

The Louisville Zoo receives about 433,000 visitors each
year. It occupies a 110-acre (45-ha) site.

The collection, in which hoofstock and the larger
cats are well-represented, includes: 54 species of
mammals (215 specimens), 57 reptiles (161 specimens), 16
amphibians (54 specimens), 75 birds (266 specimens) and
41 fish (317 specimens).

In the breeding of endangered species, the Louisville
Zoo was the first to use an embryo transfer between a
Grant's zebra and a domestic horse and has had
considerable success with woolly monkeys. Other
programs involve addax, Aruba Island rattlesnake,
Asian elephant, Bali mynah, cheetah, Dumeril's ground
boa, golden lion tamarin, guam rail, maned wolf,
ruffed lemur, Siberian tiger and white rhinoceros.

Trunkline and *Zoo Wave* are sent free of charge to
members of the zoo.

Memphis
Memphis Zoological Garden and Aquarium
2000 Galloway Avenue, Memphis,
Tennessee 38112, USA
Telephone: (901) 726-4775

Situated on 36 acres (14 ha), the Memphis Zoo receives
more than 500,000 visitors annually.

The collection, a general one featuring a variety of
antelope and reptiles, includes 72 species of mammals
(297 specimens), 94 reptiles (277 specimens), 19 amphibians (69 specimens), 101 birds (371 specimens), 84 fish
(1,220 specimens) and 10 invertebrates (24 specimens).

The zoo takes part in a number of breeding
programs under the auspices of the AAZPA. It is
studbook holder for blesbok and bontebok antelope.

Head Lions, a bimonthly newsletter, is sent to
members of the Memphis Zoological Society. The
society can be reached at the above address or phone
(901) 725-6999.

Miami
Miami Metrozoo
12400 SW 152nd Street, Miami, Florida 33177, USA
Telephone: (305) 251-0401

The Metrozoo occupies 740 acres (296 ha) and receives
about 750,000 visitors a year.

The collection is being built on zoogeographic lines.
To date, the Asian, and a portion of the African
exhibits have been developed. Included are 76 species

of mammals (267 specimens), 38 reptiles (168 specimens), 2 amphibians (3 specimens) and 152 birds
(595 specimens).

Actively engaged in breeding programs for thirty-
seven endangered or threatened species, staff at the
Metrozoo are developing a studbook for false gavial
and are participating in fifteen SSPs.

Toucan Talk, a newsletter is sent to members of the
Zoological Society of Florida, 22200 SW 152 Street,
Miami, Florida 33177, USA. Telephone: (305) 255-5551

Milwaukee
Milwaukee County Zoo
10001 W. Bluemound Road, Milwaukee, Wisconsin
53226, USA
Telephone: (414) 771-3040

Approximately 1.65 million visitors tour the Milwaukee
Zoo's 194 acres (78 ha) each year.

The collection, built on zoogeographic lines, is a
general one. It includes 95 species of mammals
(413 specimens), 58 reptiles (116 specimens), 4 amphibians (6 specimens), 38 birds (132 specimens) and
93 fish (1,326 specimens).

Among the endangered and threatened species bred
by the zoo are gorilla, bonobo, black rhinoceros, snow
leopard, Siberian tiger, ruffed lemur, Asian small-clawed
otter, clouded leopard and Humboldt penguin.
Studbooks for the giant Amazon river turtle and
cinereous vulture are kept at the zoo.

Alive magazine is distributed to members of the
Zoological Society, 10005 W. Bluemound Road,
Milwaukee, Wisconsin 53226, USA.
Telephone: (414) 258-2333.

Minneapolis–St. Paul
Minnesota Zoo
13000 Zoo Boulevard, Apple Valley,
Minnesota 55124, USA
Telephone: (612) 432-9000

About 940,000 people visit the Minnesota Zoo's
480 acres (192 ha) each year.

The collection, which emphasizes fauna of the
southeast Asian rain forests, Northern Hemisphere and
Minnesota, includes 70 species of mammals
(428 specimens), 33 reptiles (46 specimens), 5 amphibians (20 specimens), 110 birds (452 specimens) and
150 fish (252 specimens).

Apart from spacious, outdoor exhibits featuring
exotic animals, the zoo has a beaver pond, complete
with dam and lodge, so constructed that visitors can
view the animals above and below the water's surface.

The Minnesota Zoo, which is little more than a

decade old, has been committed to conservation principles from the start. It is the only zoo in the United States to successfully hatch and rear the common loon (which happens to be the Minnesota state bird). As a participant in Species Survival Plans, it breeds the Siberian tiger, Przewalski's horse, red panda, Bali mynah, lion-tailed macaque, and is studbook holder for Nigili tahr.

A zoo magazine, *Minnesota Zoo*, is distributed to members.

The Reptile House, Rodent Collection, Bronx Zoo, 1915. The epitomy of a "postage stamp" collection of animals.

New Orleans
Audubon Zoological Garden
6500 Magazine Street, New Orleans, Louisiana 70118
Telephone: (504) 861-2537

The Audubon Zoo, situated on 58 acres (23 ha), receives approximately 1 million visitors each year.

The Louisiana Swamp Exhibit, home to raccoons, nutria, black bear and alligators is a unique feature of the zoo. The collection is general. It includes: 89 species of mammals (340 specimens), 120 reptiles (383 specimens), 25 amphibians (98 specimens), 159 birds (558 specimens) and 37 fish (269 specimens).

Breeding programs are in place for such endangered species as: American red wolf, Sumatran orangutan, clouded leopard and golden lion tamarin.

A guidebook, *At the Zoo*, is available for sale to visitors at the zoo gift shop.

New York
New York Zoological Park/Bronx Zoo
Bronx, New York 10460, USA
Telephone: (212) 367-1010

In addition to the main zoo in the Bronx, which occupies 265 acres (106 ha) and receives almost 2 million visitors a year, the New York Zoological society operates the Central Park Zoo and the New York Aquarium.

The collection is broad and deep. There is a relative emphasis on Asian animals, reflecting the Society's concern for the rapid destruction of habitat in that part of the world. The collection includes 140 species of mammals (1,729 specimens), 127 species of reptiles and amphibians (697 specimens), 287 birds (977 specimens) and 250 species of fish (2,500 specimens).

The New York Zoological Society is very active in propagating endangered species. Among those receiving attention are: hooded crane, Micronesian kingfisher, Bali mynah, golden lion tamarin, lion-tailed macaque, Asian small-clawed otter, red panda, Asian elephant, several species of rhinoceros, okapi, gaur, Arabian oryx and scimitar-horned oryx. Zoo staff keep studbooks for lowland gorilla, brush-tailed bettong, white-naped crane, radiated tortoise and Chinese alligator.

Publications of the New York Zoological Society, aside from guidebooks, include *Animal Kingdom*, which is issued with membership, and *WCI News*. For information about the society, write to the address given above.

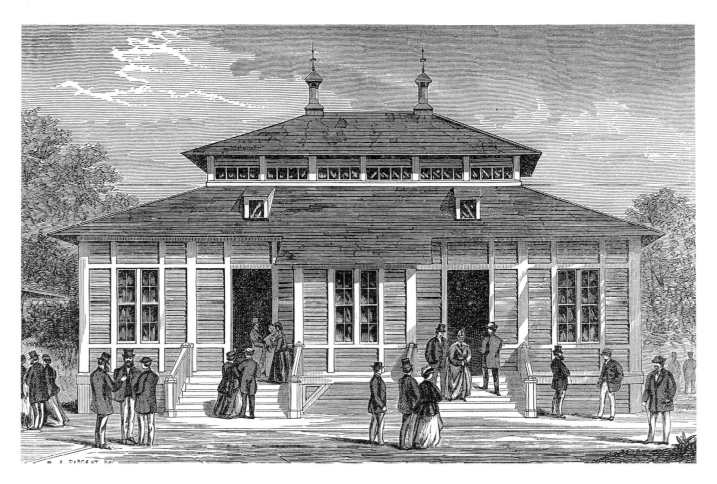

Two buildings in the Central Park Zoo in the late nineteenth century: the Temporary House for Monkeys and Birds and the Menagerie Building (opposite).

Oklahoma
Oklahoma City Zoological Park
2101 NE 50th Street, Oklahoma City, Oklahoma 73111, USA
Telephone: (405) 424-3344

Situated on 110 acres (44 ha), the zoo receives about 530,000 visitors a year.

The collection, which is strong in hoofed stock, reptiles and birds of prey, includes: 88 species of mammals (339 specimens), 117 reptiles (339 specimens), 31 amphibians (135 specimens), 137 birds (396 specimens) and 117 fish (638 specimens).

The Oklahoma Zoo participates actively in a number of SSP programs.

ZooSounds is available from the Oklahoma Zoological Society, Inc., PO Box 18424, Oklahoma City, OK 73154, USA. Telephone: (405) 427-2461.

Philadelphia
Philadelphia Zoological Garden
34th St. and Girard Ave., Philadelphia, Pennsylvania 19104, USA
Telephone: (215) 243-1100.

Each year 1.3 million people visit the zoo, which occupies 42 acres (17 ha) in the center of the city.

The considerable collection maintained by this, arguably the oldest, American zoo, includes: 109 species of mammals (504 specimens), 148 reptiles (473 specimens), 29 amphibians (61 specimens) and 167 birds (617 specimens). Great apes, waterfowl, reptiles and island species constitute areas of particular interest.

Among a number of notable exhibits in the Philadelphia Zoo is the Eleanor S. Gray Memorial Hummingbird Exhibit, a free-flight aviary, permitting remarkable views of these beautiful birds.

Endangered species bred at the zoo include the Micronesian kingfisher and Geoffrey's marmoset.

Zoo One and Zoo Too, a newsletter, is distributed as a benefit of membership in the zoological society.

Kid's stuff at the San Diego Zoo.

Pittsburgh
Pittsburgh Zoo
PO Box 5250, Pittsburgh, Pennsylvania 15206, USA
Telephone: (412) 665-3639

More than 500,000 people visit the Pittsburgh Zoo annually. It occupies 60 acres (24 ha).

The collection includes 38 species of mammals (154 specimens), 79 reptiles (273 specimens), 7 amphibians (14 specimens), 31 birds (97 specimens) and 113 fish (2,402 specimens).

The Pittsburgh Zoo is actively involved in breeding four animals listed by the AAZPA in the Species Survival Plan program: Siberian tiger, lowland gorilla, golden lion tamarin and white rhinoceros.

Animal Talk magazine is sent quarterly to Friends of the New Zoo, 6014 Penn Circle South, Pittsburgh, PA 15206, USA. Telephone (412) 441-9304.

St. Louis
St. Louis Zoological Park
Forest Park, St. Louis, Missouri 63110, USA
Telephone: (314) 781 0900

The 83-acre (33-ha) St. Louis Zoo is visited by some 2.6 million people each year.

The collection is a general one. It includes: 90 species of mammals (385 specimens), 185 reptiles (620 specimens), 50 amphibians (165 specimens), 285 birds (800 specimens) and 100 fish (500 specimens).

The St. Louis Zoo is an active participant in AAZPA sponsored SSP programs, among them: Grevy's zebra, partula snail, ruffed and black lemur and hooded crane. The zoo holds studbooks for black and ruffed lemur, hooded crane, Speke's gazelle and benteng.

A bimonthly newsletter, *Zudus*, is offered with membership in the St. Louis Zoo Friends Association.

San Antonio
San Antonio Zoo
3903 N. St. Mary's, San Antonio, Texas 78212, USA
Telephone: (512) 734-7184

The zoo occupies 50 acres (20 ha) and receives more than 900,000 visitors annually.

The collection reflects a strong curatorial interest in African antelope and birds. It includes: 136 species of mammals (752 specimens), 122 reptiles (416 specimens), 13 amphibians (40 specimens), 226 birds (1,127 specimens) and 149 fish (1,013 specimens).

The zoo is very active in propagating endangered and rare species. Among the most notable species bred at the zoo, and for which it holds studbooks, are the grizzled grey tree kangaroo, dama gazelle, toco toucan and Madagasian ground boa.

News from the Zoo, a bi-monthly newsletter, is sent to zoo members of the San Antonio Zoological Society and schools.

San Diego
San Diego Zoo and San Diego Wild Animal Park
PO Box 551, San Diego, California 92112, USA
Telephone: (619) 231-1515

The San Diego Zoo occupies 100 acres (40 ha) and is visited by 3.8 million people annually. The Wild Animal Park, also operated by the Zoological Society of San Diego, occupies 1,820 acres (728 ha) and receives approximately 1.2 million visitors annually.

The collection in San Diego includes: 226 species of mammals (1,310 specimens), 158 reptiles and amphibians (740 specimens) and 542 birds (1,894 specimens). The Wild Animal Park shelters: 119 species of mammals (1,450 specimens) and 126 birds (1,500 specimens).

Among the endangered species that are successfully reared in the zoos are koala, lemur, lion-tailed macaque, pygmy chimpanzee (bonobo), Sumatran tiger, Tahitian blue lory, kiwi and Galapagos tortoise. San Diego holds studbooks for: lemur, slender-horned gazelle, golden conure, California condor, Arabian oryx and Malayan tapir.

Subscriptions to *Zoonooz* magazine are available from the San Diego Zoo, PO Box 271, San Diego, California, 92112.

Tampa
Busch Gardens Zoological Park
PO Box 9158, Tampa, Florida 33674, USA
Telephone: (813) 988-5171

Situated on 300 acres (122 ha), Busch Gardens attracts 3.4 million visitors annually.

The collection, which features African species and South American birds, includes approximately 80 species of mammals, 20 reptiles and 240 birds, and a total of some 3,300 specimens.

Busch Gardens has achieved breeding success with a number of difficult and endangered species, among them: Asian elephant, Grevy's zebra, white tiger, scimitar-horned oryx and koala.

The Crocodile Pool in the Reptile House, Bronx Zoo, 1901. This charming space has something of the ambience of the solarium in a rich man's mansion. Such a design has the effect of domesticating, and in effect, belittling, the wild.

Appendix B: Organizations Involved in Wildlife Conservation

AMERICAN ASSOCIATION OF ZOOLOGICAL PARKS
AND AQUARIUMS
4550 Montgomery Avenue, Suite 940N, Bethesda,
Maryland 20814, USA

JERSEY WILDLIFE PRESERVATION TRUST
The Trust Secretary, Les Augrès Manor, Trinity,
Jersey, British Channel Islands
   The trust operates internationally to identify
species that are in danger of extinction, to establish
breeding programs in the wild or in captivity, and
ultimately, to return captive-bred animals to the
wild in secure conditions.

THE NATURE CONSERVANCY
1815 North Lynn Street, Arlington, Virginia
22209, USA
   The Nature Conservancy sponsors local wildlife
preserves and other chapter activities.

WILDLIFE CONSERVATION INTERNATIONAL
Membership Office, New York Zoological Society,
Bronx, New York 10460-9975, USA
   The international conservation program of the
New York Zoological Society, WCI sponsors research
and conservation projects around the world.

WORLD WILDLIFE FUND
In Australia: Level 17, St. Martin's Tower, 31st. Market
Square, GTO Box 528, Sydney, NSW 2001

In Canada: Suite 201, 60 St. Clair Avenue East,
Toronto, Ontario M4T 1N5

In Great Britain: World Wide Fund for Nature, Panda
House, Weyside Park, Godalming, Surrey GU7 1XR

In the United States: 1250 - 24th. Street N.W.,
Washington D.C. 20037

The World Wildlife Fund is the largest private
nature conservation organization in the world,
raising funds to protect endangered wildlife and wild
lands. It supports projects in 130 countries. Its top
priority is conservation of tropical rain forests in
Latin America, Asia and Africa.

ZOOLOGICAL SOCIETY OF LONDON
The Membership Department, London Zoo, Regent's
Park, London NW1 4RY, Great Britain.
   The society supports zoological research in Britain
and conservation projects abroad.

Appendix C: Glossary of Acronyms and Zoo Terms

AAZPA

American Association of Zoological Parks and
Aquariums. Headquartered at Wheeling, West
Virginia, the AAZPA has been instrumental
in coordinating breeding programs for
endangered species, particularly in North
American zoos.

ARKS

Animal Record Keeping System. A system of
computerized records devised by ISIS (see below).

AZDANZ

Association of Zoo Directors of Australia and New
Zealand. Among its other tasks, AZDANZ does some of
the same work as the AAZPA in North America,

coordinating the conservation and breeding of rare
and endangered species of zoo animals through the
Australian Species Management Scheme.

CAZPA

Canadian Association of Zoological Parks and
Aquariums

CITES

Convention on International Trade in Endangered
Species. The result of a meeting in Washington, D.C.
in 1973 to regulate and control the traffic in animals,
the convention has been signed by over a hundred
nations. The refusal of reputable zoos to take rare
animals from the wild under most circumstances is a
direct consequence of CITES.

ESSP

European Species Survival Programme. Under this program, individuals of species in the collections of participating zoos are bred according to the recommendations of a species co-ordinator, who draws on studbook data to ensure the greatest possible genetic diversity in the captive population of the endangered animal.

ISIS

International Species Inventory System.

IUCN

International Union for Conservation and Natural Resources. An independent international organization, consisting of member states and governmental and non-governmental agencies, founded in 1948 under the auspices of the United Nations. Its mission is to provide international leadership for promoting effective conservation of nature and natural resources.

IUDZG

International Union of the Directors of Zoological Gardens

NOAH

National Online Animal Histories. A database established under the auspices of the Federation of Zoological Gardens of Great Britain to provide accurate, current information about mammal and bird populations in British zoos.

Red Data Book

A comprehensive list of endangered species, together with information about their past and present distribution, compiled by the IUCN. Four volumes have been published: *Mammalia, Aves, Amphibia & Reptilia* and *Pisces.*

Species Management Scheme

Australian equivalent of ESSP and SSP.

SSP

Species Survival Plan. This program was established in 1978 by the AAZPA in support of its overall goal, to make conservation the primary purpose of zoos. Under the plan, fifty species were identified as being in imminent danger of extinction, and zoo resources were brought to bear on their rescue.

Studbook

A list of all registered specimens of a particular species of captive zoo animal, their sex, parentage, location and, where applicable, date and place of death. Its most important function is to prevent inadvertent inbreeding and to facilitate the arrangement of breeding programs that promote genetic diversity.

Interior of the Elephant House, National Zoological Park, Washington, D.C., about 1937. Most zoo exhibits are now designed to show the animal at eye level with the viewer. The pit, that tended to put the animal in an inferior position both visually and psychologically, is no less out of fashion than this slightly raised panorama, which has the effect of turning the animal into the element of an artificial picture.

Photograph Credits

The publisher would like to express appreciation to those individuals and institutions who assisted in the picture research for this book, particularly Dr. William Deiss and Susan Glenn of the Smithsonian Institution Archives in Washington, and John Edwards of London, England.

PAGE	SOURCE
6	Key Porter
10	Smithsonian Institution Archives
16	Key Porter
17	Zoo Operations Ltd., Zoological Society of London (1577/11)
18 *top*	Collection of John Edwards
18 *bottom*	Collection of John Edwards
19	Smithsonian Institution Archives
20 *top*	Field Museum of Natural History, Chicago (81164)
20 *bottom*	Smithsonian Institution
42	Collection of John Edwards (Three photographs)
92	Collection of John Edwards
126	Smithsonian Institution Archives (Mann Papers)
131	Zoo Operations Ltd., Zoological Society of London (881/PL8)
135	New York Zoological Society Photo (4036)
142	Taronga Zoo, Sydney, Australia
144	Jessie Cohen, National Zoological Park, Smithsonian Institution
162	Zoo Operations Ltd., Zoological Society of London (881/PL2)
164	Michael Silver / Photonet for the Royal Melbourne Zoological Gardens, Melbourne, Australia
169	Collection of John Edwards
170	Collection of John Edwards
171	Smithsonian Institution Archives (Mann Papers)
174	Smithsonian Institution Archives (Mann Papers)
177	Key Porter
179	New York Zoological Society Photo (2727)
181	Zoo Operations Ltd., Zoological Society of London (881/PL5)
183	New York Zoological Society Photo (7254)
184-185	Key Porter (Two pictures)
188	New York Zoological Society Photo (430)
190	Smithsonian Institution Archives
191	Smithsonian Institution Archives

Interior of the Lion House, National Zoological Park, Washington, D.C., in 1934. In designing enclosures for a species of animal nowadays, its flight distance, that is, the distance it will allow a strange animal to approach before it feels its territory has been violated and so becomes either panicky or aggressive, is taken into account. Cages such as these, in which the animal can be watched from all sides at close range, must have made the occupants extremely uncomfortable.

Suggested Reading

Robert Bendiner, *The Fall of the Wild, The Rise of the Zoo*, (New York: E.P. Dutton, 1981)

Bill Bruns, *A World of Animals: The San Diego Zoo & The Wild Animal Park*, (New York: Abrams, 1983)

Gerald Durrell, *Menagerie Manor*, (London: Hart-Davis, MacGibbon, 1964)
——————, *State of the Ark*, (New York: Doubleday, 1986)
——————, *The Stationary Ark*, (London: Collins, 1976)

Don Gold, *Zoo: A Behind-the-Scenes Look at the Animals and the People Who Care for Them*, (Chicago: Contemporary, 1988)

International Zoo Yearbook, volumes 1–27 (London: Zoological Society of London, 1960–1988)

Bernard Livingston, *Zoo: Animals, People, Places*, (New York: Arbor House, 1974)

Jon R. Luoma, *A Crowded Ark: The Role of Zoos in Wildlife Conservation*, (Boston: Houghton Mifflin, 1987)

Virginia McKenna and others, *Beyond Bars: The Zoo Dilemma*, (New York: Sterling, 1988)

National Zoological Park Staff, *Zoobook*, (Washington: Smithsonian Institution Press, 1976)

John Nichol, *New Zoos*, (New York: Christopher Helm, 1989)

Judith E. Rinard, *Zoos Without Cages*, (Washington: National Geographic Society, 1981)

John Sedgwick, *The Peaceable Kingdom: A Year in the Life of America's Oldest Zoo*, (New York: William Morrow, 1988)

Smithsonian Institution, *A Zoo for All Seasons*, (New York: Norton, 1979)

Robert Wade, *Wild in the City: The Best of Zoonooz* (San Diego: Zoological Society of San Diego, 1988)

Zoos and Aquariums in the Americas: A Directory, (American Association of Zoological Parks and Aquariums)

S. Zuckerman, *The Zoological Society of London 1826–1976 and Beyond*, (London: Academic Press, 1977)

——————, *Great Zoos of the World: Their Origins and Significance*, (London: Weidenfeld & Nicholson, 1980)